AskMen.com

PRESENTS

THE

GUY'S GUIDE
TO
ROMANCE

Other books from AskMen.com

AskMen.com Presents From the Bar to the Bedroom:
The 11 Rules for Picking up and Pleasuring Women

Askmen.com Presents The Style Bible:
The 11 Rules for Building a Complete and Timeless Wardrobe

AskMen.com

PRESENTS

THE

GUY'S GUIDE
TO
ROMANCE

THE 11 RULES FOR FINDING

A WOMAN AND

MAKING HER HAPPY

EDITED BY JAMES BASSIL

Collins

An Imprint of HarperCollins*Publishers*

Portions of this book have previously appeared on the AskMen.com website.

Contributors:

Armando Gomez	Jessica Lloyd	Joanne O'Neill
Ian Harrison	Gary Jackson	Ashkan Karbasfrooshan
Daniel Harrison	Ross Bonander	Tamara Hanson
Sabrina Rogers	Kyle Darbyson	Shaina Falcone
Ricardo Poupada	Kristen Armstrong	Michael Hirsch
Karin Eldor	Stephanie Eldred	Dario Palombi
Luis Rodrigues	Allison Young	Jon Platner
Rosy Saadeh	Andy Levy-Ajzenkopf	Daniel Ehrenfeld
Chris Rovny	Stefanie Stiles	
Lisa Iwanycki	Andrea Gourgy	

HarperCollins books may be purchased for educational, business, or sales promotional use. For information, please write: Special Markets Department, HarperCollins Publishers, 10 East 53rd Street, New York, NY 10022.

FIRST EDITION

Designed by Jaime Putorti

Library of Congress Cataloging-in-Publication Data

AskMen.com presents the guy's guide to romance : the 11 rules for finding a woman and making her happy / edited by James Bassil.—1st ed.
    p. cm.
  ISBN 978-0-06-124286-1
  1. Dating (Social customs). 2. Man–woman relationships. 3. Courtship. 4. Mate selection. I. Bassil, James. II. AskMen.com.
  HQ801.A8225 2008
  646.7'7081—dc22   2007028824

10 /QGP 10 9 8 7 6 5 4 3 2

CONTENTS

Contents

INTRODUCTION

For all the differences that exist between the genders—and there are plenty—men and women are still united in one common pursuit: that of each other. Every guy is looking for that special woman, and every woman is looking for that special guy . . . so you'd think that we'd all have an easy time getting together. As most of us learn the hard way, however, securing a great and satisfying romantic relationship is anything but easy. In fact, it's bloody hard work.

For men, a great deal of this difficulty is navigational. Lacking the instinct for relationships and the natural propensity for analyzing them that women have, most of us guys don't even know which romantic approaches are the right ones. Even those of us with great dating track records aren't sure how we accumulated them. Initial meetings seemed the product of coincidence or luck, maintenance a question of reaction, and the final demise an inevitability. With few lessons learned, the transition to the next relationship can feel like another stumble and flounder-about, rather than a successfully managed operation.

Of course, relationships aren't clinical affairs that can be micromanaged; they're evolving, ever-changing entities. But there are certain consistent rules and patterns that underlie all of them, and an understanding of these forces can help transform your actions in a partnership from guesswork to well-informed strategy. Approaching a relationship in this seemingly calculating manner may seem cold, but it's simply a matter of making the best of a good thing.

Every man's first step in embarking on the successful pursuit of romance is accepting this imperative of taking action and informing oneself—you've already acknowledged as much by picking up this book. From here, we'll take you through all steps of a successful relationship, starting with the precursor to it: meeting her. After summarizing the key points of the pickup and pursuit stage (which we covered in detail in a previous book, *From the Bar to the Bedroom*), we'll take you through the coordination and execution of perfect dates, how to evaluate your compatibility, how to meet her friends, and how to manage the transition into a long-term relationship. Then we'll plunge into the meatier relationship issues: handling arguments and jealousy issues, meeting her family, moving in together, and planning out and pursuing a future together.

Every new romantic relationship carries with it the potential to develop into one of the most valuable elements of a man's life. Let's give your next one the chance to fulfill its potential by taking you through our crash course, *The Guy's Guide to Romance*.

RULE 1
MEET HER

Before any romance can blossom, there has to be an initial meeting, and before there can be an initial meeting, there has to be a guy willing to step up and initiate contact—and that guy is you. Is it possible that she'll be the one to pick *you* up? Sure, anything's possible, but it's not likely. And while you're sitting around waiting for it to happen, plenty of other guys will be making their moves, and plenty of happy coupledoms will be emerging for it.

Like it or not, it still falls on the man to initiate the pursuit, and that isn't likely to change anytime soon. Rather than lamenting this fact, it's time to adapt to it. Begin by conquering that fear that inhibits so many men from approaching women: the fear of rejection.

OVERCOME YOUR FEAR OF REJECTION

Mankind has overcome the hardships of war and natural disasters. Yet there is one natural fear that seems to overcome most men: the fear of rejection. This instinctive emotion paralyzes us and hinders us from doing the things we really want to do, including meeting women. Some men are so afraid of rejection that they would rather run through a minefield than walk up to a woman and ask her out on a date.

You're not her type

Most men fear rejection because it lowers their self-esteem. But there is really no reason to lose any confidence when women say "no" because they aren't really rejecting you. How could they be rejecting you when they don't even know what you're all about? It's not like they studied your personality and qualities before deciding to refuse you. Maybe they declined your offer because:

- They're dating someone or married.

- They're having a bad day.

- They like you, but have their protective shield up.

- They don't feel like talking to anyone—even Brad Pitt.

The important thing to remember is that no one in this world can appeal to everyone's tastes. Each woman has her preferences, so if she rejects you, it just means that you don't fit the description of what she desires. All the more reason to approach as many women as possible in order to increase your chances of finding one who is looking for a guy like you.

TAKE THE PLUNGE

The "fear of rejection" will persist until the day you decide to overcome it. All you have to do is start up a conversation, and the rest will fall into place. Note that this does *not* involve corny pickup lines. An honest conversation is the best route. Here are some suggestions.

■ Once you notice signs that she's interested (eye contact, touching her hair, and so on), walk directly up to her and introduce yourself. You can start by asking if you can join her for a drink. If she says yes, ask her name. If she's interested, she'll ask the same. If she doesn't ask, it's not the end of the world; just keep the lines of communication open.

■ Keep the conversation interesting; focus on her and really listen to what she says. Then, follow up with another question that links with what she just finished saying. For example:

> YOU: "Do you have a job?"
>
> HER: "Yes, and I'm also studying."
>
> YOU: "Wow, you're a busy woman!"
>
> HER: "Yes, there are days when I feel like I'm just going to collapse."
>
> YOU: "I bet you're looking forward to a vacation."
>
> HER: "Oh yes, I just can't wait to get away for a while."
>
> YOU: "And what would your ideal vacation spot be?"

This is just one example of many possible conversations. The idea is to listen to her and follow up with a correlating question. When this method is properly applied, it will keep the conversation interesting.

TOP 10 ICEBREAKERS

Of course, striking up a conversation with a beautiful stranger is easier said than done. It helps to have some tried-and-true ways to break the ice and start a conversation up your sleeve.

Whether you're at work, play, or somewhere in between, there are always opportunities to meet women. It's just a matter of knowing the right thing to say at the right time to come across as cool, honest, and intriguing. You'll strike out from time to time, but that's okay. Don't dwell on rejection. Stay confident, and you'll be meeting more women than you know what to do with.

Your main weapon is always the art of adaptation. Before moving in, assess whether the scenario involves a "hot" or a "cold" pickup.

- Hot situations occur when she's noticed you and has given you that "come hither" signal (either via eye contact, a sexy flip of her hair, or one of those shy smiles).

- Cold situations, on the other hand, happen when there hasn't been any previous flirting. This scenario can prove to be more difficult, as you're never sure if she is, or will be, interested.

Number 10: Introduce yourself

This almost goes without saying: If there has been no previous flirting, she's not going to know you exist until you make her aware you're there. To use a golf analogy, it's always the approach shot that sets up the hole. No different with the ladies. Stride up to her casually and introduce yourself.

What to say:

"I'm Joe, happy to meet you."
"I'm Joe. I don't believe we've been introduced."

Number 9: Buy her a drink

Whether you're at a bar, restaurant, or coffee shop, a great icebreaker involves the classic buying of a drink. Have the waiter send her another round of what she's already having (if you want to be more aggressive, you could send her your favorite drink), accompanied by a playful note, with your phone number included. Be sure to have the waiter let her know the source of the drink. On your way out, stop by her table and introduce yourself. It's a bold approach, without being invasive.

What to say:

> "Hope you enjoyed your drink."
> "This is my favorite drink; thought you might enjoy it too."

Number 8: Ask if she's single

Hey, you're going to want to know at some point, so why not get it over with at the outset? Keep in mind, however, that this is a bold move in any situation. If you're a handsome guy, the chances that she'll react positively are obviously better. If you're not, it's all the more reason to be friendly. In any case, this approach always demands that you be direct. You can bet that she will be; if she tells you that she's not single, or if she's not interested, you'll find out quickly. Asking a stranger if she's available immediately reveals your intentions and eliminates the chances of awkward misunderstandings.

What to say:

> "Before I even ask your name, I need to know: are you single?"
> "Could I be so lucky that you're single?"

Number 7: Be blunt

Here's an approach for those willing to be even more direct. In many cases, walking up to a woman and letting her know you're a take-charge kind of guy can carry a strong appeal. She'll likely take your confidence as an indication that you're someone worth talking to.

What to say:

"I was trying to think of a clever pickup line, but then realized there's no such thing. My name is Joe. What's yours?"

"Mind if I join you?"

Number 6: Comment on your surroundings

Wherever you may find her, there will always be stuff around to observe. Use it as conversational fodder. Look to your environment to induce a positive conversation and gently ease it toward common topics. This strategy needn't be restricted to the nightlife; if you notice a woman having a bad day at the office, say something that will make her forget her drudgery. This allows her to vent and capitalizes on the setting to get the conversation rolling. Be sure, however, that she's not seriously busy before you move in. Pick your timing as carefully as you do your prey.

What to say:

"I've heard this DJ somewhere else, he sounds great."

"You look like you're having a great day." (Said with sarcasm if she looks bored or unhappy.)

Number 5: Ask an open-ended question

The hardest part of using an icebreaker is employing it to start a conversation that doesn't end thirty seconds after it's begun. Avoid this scenario by asking her a question that requires some kind of elaboration in the response, and not simply a "yes" or "no."

What to say:

"So, what do you do for fun?"

"So, how do you keep busy on weekends?"

Number 4: Have her buy you a drink

Throw a twist into your icebreaker by using a little gender role-reversal. If you find yourself in a hot situation at a bar or club, approach her and ham it up a little. It should surprise her in a mischievous way, and can be charming. Although riskier, this approach might also work in a cold situation.

What to say:

"I'll tell you what, how about I let you buy me a drink?"

"I've always felt that it's a bit chauvinistic to offer to buy a woman a drink. So I'll let you buy me one and promise to repay the favor."

Number 3: Give a sincere compliment

It's no secret that women enjoy compliments. However, they can always detect when the compliment is an insincere one. No matter the situation, you should always be able to find something unique and legitimate to flatter your target with. It may be risqué or a more tame form of praise, depending on her body language toward you. Be sure to follow through with a negative hit, so that she doesn't believe that you're in awe over her.

What to say:

"It's funny that you noticed that . . . you're very perceptive."

"You have a nice, sugary laugh."

What is a negative hit? Think of it as a playful, lighthearted insult or tease, delivered to the beautiful woman in lieu of the clichéd compliment she usually hears. In other words, it's the last thing she expects to hear, but the one thing she'll remember at the end of the night. If you fawn all over her and never give her a dose of reality, she will quickly grow tired of your overly positive chatter. Hot women don't need another fan club member; they need a challenge. Breaking up conversation with the odd negative hit or tease (adapted to her personality, of course) will tell her she can also speak her mind freely. Then watch the sparks fly.

Number 2: Say "hello"

As obvious as it seems, this classic approach is often overlooked. Most women will say it right back, if only because it's common courtesy to do so. Their acknowledgement, however, opens the door to more conversation. It's a simple, no-nonsense approach, and just mustering the courage to greet a stranger may win you some respect. This approach works in virtually any setting.

What to say:

"Hi."
"Hello."

Number 1: Make her smile

Getting her to smile works magic for breaking the ice; women love a man who can make them laugh. Cracking a joke could prove the difference between picking up and striking out. Humor sets up a pleasant context and hints that you're a fun guy.

What to say:

"I bet I can make you smile in five seconds."
"Want to hear a really bad pickup line?"

LEARN TO READ A WOMAN'S BODY LANGUAGE

Most people think that in the courting game, men are the first to initiate the courtship. But that is completely incorrect. The reality is that in almost all successful pickups, it is the woman who seduces the man—without saying a single word.

In other words, a woman will initiate the game by using body language to signal that she is interested, available, and receptive. By reading a woman's physical lingo, you can spot a woman across the room who's either single and looking, taken but unhappy, aching to satisfy her sexual needs, or simply wanting to engage in a pleasant conversation.

Read her body, not her mind

Most gentlemen fail to realize the importance of body language. Instead, they try to focus on reading a woman's mind. They stand around for hours with a drink in their hands, wondering if she's interested or not. Little do they know, but the answer lies in her stance.

Forget about trying to read her mind. Stop trying to read her thoughts and look at her body instead. Note that in this context, the word "body" refers not to her breasts, but rather to her flirtatious behavior and gestures, i.e., her facial and posture patterns.

Unfortunately, men usually either choose to completely ignore a woman's body language or are completely clueless as to how to interpret the signs. But remember this—everything about socializing is based on the following two facts:

First, communication is 60% nonverbal. Second, nonverbal signs have five times more impact than verbal ones. So if you're not paying attention to her body language, you're missing out on 60% of the game.

Basic stages of nonverbal communication

Learning to read a woman's body language is a simple three-stage process. The first stage reveals whether she's interested in you, and helps you to decide if you should approach her or not.

The second stage allows you to see if she's receptive to your courtship, or whether she is beginning to feel uncomfortable with you. This is the crucial stage; you have to really observe her comfort and level of interest and adjust your whole approach based on that.

The third stage gives you a pretty good idea of whether you should close the deal, or move on without further wasting your time. Should you exchange phone numbers, plan a date, or invite her back to your place? Look deeply at her posture and she will let you know.

Stage 1: The Approach

Okay, so you've been standing around the room for the past 2.3 hours and you're still wondering if the beautiful redhead is attracted to you.

Well, get off your feet and start observing her; look for the clues mentioned in the table below. If you get the signs, don't hesitate; trust your feelings and walk up to her. When women are not interested, they simply look down and don't focus on you. If she's gazing at you, then she's interested. But don't get all excited and make a mess in your pants; this only means that she finds you attractive, not that she wants you as a boyfriend. The game has just begun.

SHE'S INTERESTED	DON'T BOTHER
Sidelong glance	*Never sneaks a peek*
First looks down, then away to the side	*Looks away at eye level*
Looks at you for a few minutes	*Fleeting eye contact*
Holds your gaze briefly	*Looks away quickly*
Posture changes to alert	*Posture unchanged*
Tilted head	*Vertical head*
Matches your posture	*Posture unchanged*
Thrusts breasts	*Sags breasts*
Does not touch face, touches hair	*Does not touch hair, touches face, nose, and ears*

Stage 2: The Maintenance and Repair

Sure, you've made eye contact, and your introduction was flawless, but you still don't know a thing about the woman you're talking to. That's why it's crucial to analyze how she reacts around you and to the words that come out of your mouth.

Use the following signs to help adjust your conversation and pickup strategy in order to make her feel more comfortable around you (calming her fears is the key to a successful pickup). This will ensure that she sticks around for the grand finale.

KEEP TALKING	START WALKING
Alert and energetic	*Tense and restless*
Open posture	*Remains closed*
Lowers drink	*Keeps drink at chest level*
Caresses objects (cup)	*Taps objects*
Loosens everything	*Tightens anything*
Leans forward	*Leans away*

Stage 3: The Closure

Finally, you don't want to be one of the millions of men who dare to approach a woman but forget to close the deal. Sometimes, a woman is begging to exchange numbers, see you again, or even sleep with you. Look for the Take Me Home signs. Or, move on and don't waste your time if you're getting the Only Being Polite signs.

TAKE ME HOME	ONLY BEING POLITE
Keeps eyes on you	*Looks around room*
Smiles—shows teeth	*Smiles slightly*
Puts anything in mouth	*Nothing goes in mouth*
Turns body toward you	*Keeps facing away*
Looks at you while drinking	*Looks away and drinks*
Touches you	*Does not touch you*

Paying attention and observing body language is the secret to successfully meeting women. A man who knows this will always have women around him for the picking.

ALWAYS GET HER PHONE NUMBER

Positive and inviting body language will be of little value to you unless you use it as a cue to take action. Having established that there is a mutual attraction, you can't just sit around and wait for a relationship to magically materialize. Nor can you expect her to pull the trigger and set things into motion. On top of taking the initiative to set up contact, women also expect the man to close the deal (i.e., to get her phone number).

Unfortunately, however, many men shy away from doing just that. When the time comes to close the deal, they all too often settle with a simple, "It was nice meeting you," then walk home kicking themselves.

Why would you go through all that anxiety and work to begin the process of pitching yourself as a potential romantic interest, only to end up with no sale at all?

Ask for her number

You should get into the habit of asking for a number every time you approach a woman—even if you don't plan on calling her. The more you do this, the less intimidating the act will be, and the more it will become second nature to you.

You should also get into the habit of approaching your goal (to secure her number) as a strategic routine, which we will presently break down for you. You can use this strategy anywhere, including clubs, restaurants, libraries, and cafés. And if she doesn't give you her number, you'll learn how to bow out without feeling embarrassed. But before we ask for numbers, let's understand the factors that will influence whether a woman gives you her number, or gives you the 555 routine.

Female psychology 101

Most women are reluctant to give out their numbers for several reasons, the most important of which is safety, or lack thereof. The last thing a woman wants is to hand over an invitation for a stalker to jump on her bandwagon. So, before she even considers sharing numbers with you, you'll have to pass a couple of tests.

If a man looks desperate, she'll think there is definitely something wrong with him. Desperate men tend to become stalkers. Instead, show that you're confident.

Too many compliments—especially generic ones—will alert her to the possibility that you're trying too hard to get something out of her. You can bet that she will be a little more vigilant while you're around. Keep compliments moderate and a little more original and unique to her.

The Rules of the Game

1. Ignore Friends

Make sure your friends aren't hanging around looking your way and making faces like, "You're the man." Good wingmen take their roles seriously and don't act like children by stealing their Wing Commander's thunder.

2. Exchange Numbers

Never give your number without taking hers. Never take her number without giving yours. If she doesn't want to give you her number, move on.

3. Right Words

Never ask for a number. This makes you look wimpy, as if you're begging for it. Instead, look directly into her eyes and request it in a way that sounds as if you're *expecting* her to give the number. Don't give her the option of saying no. You can use phrases like:

> *I've had a really nice time talking to you, and I don't know if*
> *I'll run into you again. Let's exchange numbers so that we can*
> *do this again another time.*

> *You know, you're a very interesting person to talk to. I'd love*
> *for you to have my number and I'd love to have yours as well,*
> *so that we can have an opportunity to speak again.*

In both cases, the idea is to imply that you are going to give her your phone number and that she will give hers in return. Do not ask her whether it's okay with her—just presume that it is. At this point, she'll either give you her number or an excuse.

4. Be Unprepared

Don't take out a pen and a piece of paper to write her number. You'll look like someone who planned the whole situation. Women like spontaneous men who act in the moment.

Instead, discreetly ask someone (bartender) for a pen and use available props such as a matchbook or napkin.

5. Give Her the Pen

Don't write the phone number yourself; give her the opportunity to write it down. Ask her to write her full name. This will prevent the embarrassing, "I'm sorry, what's your name again?" situation (a big mistake) from happening.

6. Leave

As soon as you get the number, leave her presence. This will serve two purposes. First, you aren't sticking around and risking the chance of ruining the good impression you've made. Second, you'll leave her wanting more.

7. Remember Details

Once you find yourself alone, remember the details of the conversation and write them down so that you can use them when you call her, and show that you actually listened to her.

8. No Celebration

Once you get her number, return to your wingmen without performing a victory dance and high-fiving your buddies. Women find this kind of celebration very unattractive, and you'll be having a relationship with her voice mail until you get the hint.

9. No Excuses

If, instead of giving you her number, she begins to make an excuse, don't wait for her to finish. Simply interrupt her with, "It was nice meeting you," and walk away.

That's right, boys, don't give her the benefit of shooting you down. This is where you look confident and walk away with your head held up high. Don't even wait for her reaction, just walk away and go find someone else.

She says: "I'm just so busy with work right now."

She means: I am not interested in fitting you into my schedule.

Why she does this: She wants to let you down easy. Instead of being blunt, she is hoping you'll just get the picture.

What you should do: When a woman likes a man, she will always find time for him—no matter what her schedule is like. So don't kid yourself into thinking that the situation might change. Instead, move on right away.

7 GOLDEN RULES FOR PHONE CALLS

So you've finally scored a phone number from that girl you've been working up the nerve to approach. You know how important the first telephone conversation will be, and your nerves are rattled.

So now what? Telephone etiquette is a central part of the general impression you give a woman. Indeed, many disastrous conversations could be avoided if more people would simply think before dialing. So if you are rusty or telephonically challenged, or even if you have been playing the field regularly, it can't hurt to fine-tune your game. While most supposed dating experts will give you dozens of telephone strategies to follow, we at AskMen.com prefer to keep things simple. The seven tips below are all you need to develop a polished telephone personality and make a killer first impression.

1. Keep conversations short

Whether you are a busy corporate attorney, self-employed, or even unemployed, you always want to give her the impression that you lead a full, active life. By keeping your initial telephone conversations brief, you will give her the impression that you are busy and in demand. And as an added bonus, if you are always the one ending the conversations, it will keep you in a position of control, leaving her wanting more and more of your time.

2. Leave on a high note

She'll always remember what you said last. Therefore, before ending a conversation, make an effort to leave on a positive note, such as with a well-thought-out joke or a funny story. Even if your entire telephone conversation went poorly, if you leave her smiling before saying goodbye, she is more likely to want to speak to you again—and hopefully see you in person.

3. Have a purpose for your call

Don't just call to chitchat. We cannot stress this enough: preparation, preparation, preparation. Be armed and ready with a purpose for your call (the most likely purpose being to ask her out, of course); this will give her the impression that you are assertive and thoughtful enough to think of a plan beforehand. This plan will also serve as a backup should there be an awkward silence in the conversation.

4. Be positive

Women might have the reputation of being natural listeners, but the truth is that she probably won't stick around if you're all about gloom and negativity. It doesn't matter if your boss is disrespectful or your co-worker is incompetent—complaints are a real turnoff, especially in the early stages. You can avoid looking needy by keeping your emotional baggage to yourself, at least at the beginning. Make a concerted effort to keep all conversations positive and the griping to a minimum.

5. Leave a message only on the second call

You should avoid leaving a message on the first call; it may make you seem too needy. Herein lies perhaps the most important, and least flexible, of all the rules: Do not think that you will elude her radar by calling from an unknown number or hanging up on her machine numerous times. If she doesn't answer your first call, feel free to hang up without leaving a message and try again later. Upon the second phone call, leave a message, and *don't call again until she does.* By not calling more than twice, you not only avoid the dreaded appearance of desperation, but you also throw the ball into her court and get the chance to gauge her interest in you (by seeing when or if she calls you back).

6. Place the call at an appropriate time

Phone calls during working hours are a complete no-no. First, you'll be busted for daydreaming about her on the job—if you take time off from work to call her, she'll know she's very much on your mind. Second, she might not be as receptive to your phone call with her co-workers or boss in her midst. If you'd like to set up a date for the weekend, call by Wednesday.

Avoid Friday and Saturday night phone calls at all costs; even if you are at home with your dog watching a movie, she doesn't need to know that.

7. Leave coherent messages

Don't leave long, rambling messages on her voicemail. Picture this: Every message you leave on her voicemail could potentially be played back and analyzed several times over. Your tone and choice of wording could be used as points of discussion with her friends. Therefore, your best defense against a disastrous message is brevity. Identify yourself by name (especially in the early stages of getting to know her, don't just say, "It's me"), then get to the point. Leave one phone number where you can be reached, but don't leave your work number, e-mail, and so on—this will just seem desperate.

Rules for dating success

Why introduce steadfast telephone rules into the world of dating? If you haven't already been convinced by what you've read, the answer is very simple: you achieve better results.

Many of us—men and women alike—who are in pursuit of a romantic interest have a tendency to forget about rules and follow our hearts. Sadly, even good intentions can result in countless unanswered calls and, consequently, a severe blow to one's confidence and dignity. All this can be avoided if you are consistent about implementing the above tips. Within no time, your sophisticated telephone persona will surely stir her curiosity, and she'll be eager to hear more of your voice—in person. It's time to set up your first date.

RULE 2
BE A FIRST DATE PRO

anding yourself a first date is only the first step in securing a smooth transition into an eventful and exciting night. A first date is about making a strong impression. A woman wants to feel that the man she's with has not only thought about the date, but has also prepared accordingly.

7 THINGS WOMEN EXPECT ON A FIRST DATE

Here are some tips to help you decipher her unspoken expectations for the evening and figure out what she wants you to do but would never actually say.

1. Go the extra mile . . . or two

If you greet her with a red rose and a smile, you're sure to get a warm response. But why not turn up the heat and offer her a less stereotypical treat? If you already know some details about this woman, use the information to your advantage. If her favorite color is purple, give her a purple flower. Otherwise, use your imagination. The key is creativity—she'll be impressed if you've shown that you not only got her something, but that you thought about her while doing it.

2. Be polite, not pushy

She may not tell you that etiquette is a priority, but you can be sure that she's keeping an eye on what you are and, perhaps more important, what you aren't doing. It's the little details that make the difference, like chewing with your mouth closed. Remember: Nothing you have to say is either important or funny enough that it can't be said after you swallow.

Do offer to open the door for her, but if she insists on doing it herself, let her. And keep the conversation polite as well. Remember: Any stories that involve vomit or secretions of any sort (no matter how funny or appropriate you think they are) run the risk of being a complete turnoff.

3. Be complimentary

Many men forget to notice and compliment their date on her appearance. There must be something about her outfit, her hair, or the way she smells that you like. You can rest assured that she's spent a good portion of her time primping and preparing for this first date, and it's important that you acknowledge her efforts.

4. Be curious about her

You're nervous and trying to make sure that she thinks you're better (and more original) than the last guy who showed up at her door. The result can often be you talking about all the things you've accomplished while neglecting to ask her about her interests. Your intentions might be to keep the conversation flowing, but a monologue actually makes for a more uncomfortable evening than a few awkward pauses. So be sure to ask her about herself; just don't turn it into an interview.

5. Be assertive, not aggressive

It's important that you show her you're confident. It's also important not to blur the line between being assertive and being aggressive while interacting with her, as well as with those who might even prove to be allies on your first date. When dealing with your waiter, she'd prefer you be courteous rather than cantankerous. If what you order isn't what you get, then by all means tell your waiter, but don't raise your voice and demand that it be taken back. A polite smile and a simple assertion that your order has been confused is the perfect time for you to show your willingness to forgive while your waiter tries to make it up to you (all the while making you look even better). Likewise, if the movie you both wanted to see is sold out, take it in good humor and, most important . . .

6. Always have a backup plan

If the plans you made unravel at the last moment, relax. You can always rely on plan B to make the most of what might have been a wasted night. She'll either be impressed by your on-the-spot creativity or glowing at the thought of you considering a "just in case" scenario for your date. It doesn't have to be overly extravagant, just make sure you have some other ideas in the event the night doesn't come together exactly as planned. From ice-skating to salsa dancing to coffee drinking—any backup option is better than no option at all.

7. Leave her impressed

The evening seems to be coming to a close; it's time to pull that proverbial ace from up your sleeve. You want to leave her with a lasting impression about what a wonderful time she had and how lucky she was to spend it with you. Seeing her to her door may likely get you further than the front door. But give her the option to welcome you in by taking it one step at a time. Offering a polite end to a wonderful evening just leaves her wanting more and gives her the chance to assert herself if she's craving more than a kiss at night's end.

TOP 10 FIRST DATE CONVERSATION TIPS

Learning the basic first date rules may ensure that she remembers you as a cordial and thoughtful gentleman, but it won't help much in the way of actually passing the time. And no matter what kind of activity you have planned for your meeting, what she's most likely to remember about it will be your head-to-head chats. Part of what makes a woman want a second date is an engaging, natural conversation on the first one. Don't know where to begin? Have no fear. The following ten tips will keep the conversation flowing smoothly.

Number 10: Avoid her romantic past

One should never ask about past lovers on a first date. In fact, this should be avoided until she initiates the topic (if she ever does). She might have been hurt or she may still be in love with her ex. It's best to start with a clean slate. The goal is to take off her lipstick by the end of the evening, not help her wipe away the tears as they smudge her mascara.

Number 9: Brothers or sisters

Usually, a safe topic of conversation is asking about siblings (don't ask her if she's got cute sisters). Again, asking about her parents could backfire if they experienced a divorce or separation, especially if it happened when she was young. But sisters and brothers usually trigger good feelings and score points for you since you're showing a caring side and an interest in her family life.

Number 8: Travel

A tricky way to spark a girl's interest is by asking about her past travel destinations and where she plans to travel in the future. This provides both people with some insight into each other's interests, cultural background, and openness to new adventures.

Number 7: Drinks and food

A good topic for conversation, especially if the date is taking place at a restaurant or bar, is the kind of food and drink each of you likes. Again, not only can you gauge whether or not you share culinary preferences, but the potential topics are endless and provide you with a safe topic of conversation.

Number 6: Past education and future plans

Asking a girl about her past education and whether she intends to return to school is admittedly risky. She might love to go on and on about her numerous academic achievements, or she might break down and admit that her current job has absolutely nothing to do with what she studied. In either case, you are provided with a golden opportunity for a thought-provoking discussion.

Number 5: Career

If you are years removed from your college days, then talking about work and career goals just might be a safer topic. Admittedly, you should not let her go into the mundane details about how fed up she is with her life (which would explain why she's on her seventh margarita). But generally speaking, people like to brag about work, no matter how routine it is. It also gives you an idea regarding whether or not you are dating a future CEO or a waitress for life.

Number 4: Friends

Ask her about her friends. Even if you do not know them, she will love to tell you about her circle of friends, how much they mean to her, and where she met them (and all of the things they did together). Don't doze off, though; this is when you get precious details about her via the kind of people she surrounds herself with.

Number 3: Free time

Does she do yoga or dance? How about sports? What kind of music does she like? These are the questions you must ask to determine how much of a bond exists between the two of you. Moreover, you will gain some insight into potential follow-up questions.

Number 2: Weekend plans

By sharing your typical weekend leisure plans, you will get a clearer picture of what life with her would be like if you were hanging out on a day-to-day basis. By not specifically including her in your plans, you are also sending mixed messages; you are showing that your private social life is a priority, which is not entirely bad at first. Yes, mind games are childish, but keeping your cards at your chest gives you leverage. She will ask herself, "will he want to see me on weekends?"

Number 1: Be bold and look ahead

If her body language is positive, you can look ahead and talk about other things you could do together in the future. Admittedly, you do not want to rush too far ahead and scare her off, but if she's enjoying herself, chances are she'll be curious to see what other great adventures you have in store for her.

TIPS FOR A BLIND DATE

Not all first dates are the product of successful first meetings. In fact, some first dates actually *are* the first meetings. Regardless of whether you were set up by a friend or met online or through a personal ad, blind dates can be exciting and unnerving at the same time. A blind date is a unique experience, and while many general dating tips hold true, these special circumstances require special measures. After all, what if she's ugly? What if she's crazy? What if she doesn't show up?

From picking the location to making conversation, here are some tips to get you ready for a blind date.

The location

Choose a crowded location

Make sure there are a lot of people. She'll feel at ease, and you'll be able to exit quickly and easily if you need to.

Pick a neutral location

Choose a place where everyone doesn't know your name, but be somewhat familiar with it so you look like you know what you're talking about when ordering a drink.

Make a date for cocktails

If the date isn't going well, you won't have the obligation of sitting through an entire meal; you can make up an excuse after the first drink and leave.

Arrive separately

Meet up at the chosen location. She'll probably feel more comfortable if you don't show up at her place before you've met, and you'll be able to leave whenever you like.

The meeting

Let her take the lead during introductions

She may shake your hand or move right in to give you a quick peck on the cheek. The ball is in her court.

Don't order food right away

If the date is going badly, you won't be stuck with the food commitment. If things are going well, order something that you can share, like some nachos or a plate of assorted appetizers.

Pay the bill

Yes, she wants to be treated equally, but she may still have an old-fashioned side that believes the man should pay on the first date. So don't ask her for half; just cough up the cash.

Don't push yourself on her

Blind dates are touchy and need to be handled carefully. She has no idea what type of person you are. For all she knows, you could be a stalker. Don't touch her if you aren't sure whether it's appropriate. If you touch her too soon, she'll think you're creepy. Let her initiate the physical contact.

The end

Start making plans for the next date

If the date went well and you had fun, tell her. If you'd like to see her again, let her know.

Leave on a positive note

You don't need to make this a blind date marathon. Hanging out for a couple of hours is sufficient. The important thing is to have fun. If there is chemistry, great. If there isn't, just let it go. There are more blind dates where this one came from.

Be clear

Make sure there's no confusion, even if you are uninterested. Saying misleading or vague things like "I'll call you" or "Let's call each other" makes you sound insincere.

What if . . .

She doesn't show up for the blind date?

Wait no more than twenty minutes and leave. Don't call her to find out why she's late; she should be calling you. If she's late for your first date, she's probably not worth sticking around for.

The date is a flop?

Be upfront and tell her the date isn't working out. Don't tell her you'll call her when you know you won't. Thank her for coming, say goodbye and leave.

She brings a friend along?

You are either being checked out or given the brush-off. Either way, go along with it and see what happens. If she's making conversation with her friend rather than with you, then she isn't worth the time. If her attention is completely on you, then call a friend to come and join you. He can take care of her girlfriend, while you enjoy your blind date.

TOP 10 FIRST DATE FAUX PAS

Women are harsh critics, especially on a first date. They're analyzing your clothing, your table manners, what you say, and what you don't say.

If you want to pass the test (and advance to date number two), be sure not to commit any of these top ten first date crimes.

Number 10: Being a knight in shining armor

You pick up your date and hand her a dozen red roses. "Your chariot awaits," you say as you race ahead to get the car door for her . . . the first of many doors. In your world, chivalry is not dead—it's very much alive and requires you to open every single door for her. Well, sorry to shatter your Prince Charming dreams, but women don't expect you to be a doorman. In fact, this can be downright annoying. Of course, they don't want a ignorant fool who shovels food into his mouth, talks with his mouth full, and keeps his elbows on the table, either. That's just plain rude (and a major turnoff). What women do want is something in between: not a knight in shining armor or a slob, but a gentleman.

Number 9: Choosing a bad venue

You've offered to pick the restaurant, so which one do you choose?

a) Fast food joint

b) Happy hour at Hooters

c) Fancy schmancy restaurant (where entrées start at fifty dollars)

d) None of the above

If you answered d) None of the above, give yourself a pat on the back. That's the winning ticket. The other options serve a purpose, but they're not appropriate first date venues. A fast food joint tells her you're cheap, Hooters tells her you're a pervert (even though they do have great wings), and fancy schmancy tells her you're a showoff. Women want something that's not too cheap and not too expensive, but just right—a place that falls in between fancy and cheap, so that it doesn't look like you're trying too hard or like you're not trying hard enough.

Number 8: Being wishy-washy

When she asks where you want to go for dinner, you hem and haw and eventually say, "Doesn't matter." And then at dinner, you spend hours deliberating over the menu and end up asking the waitress what she recommends. Wrong and wrong. Women don't want a spineless guy who can't make a decision to save his life. They want backbone, direction, and confidence. In fact, some women rate confidence higher than appearance and sense of humor, so make sure you show her you've got lots of it—just avoid being overly confident to the point of arrogance.

Number 7: Getting transfixed by TV

You're listening intently as she goes on about her sister who just got accepted to the Peace Corps and her brother who's doing his Master's in chemical engineering. While you're honestly enthralled by the conversation, you briefly glance at the TV perched behind the bar for one teeny tiny second . . . and you get busted! You might not think it's a big deal (come on, you barely looked), but to her it's huge. Why? Because even though you were listening intently, she takes your sneak peek as a screaming sign that you're not interested. There goes date number two. The easiest way to avoid the TV trap is by not picking a place with TVs in the first place, and if you do wind up at a sports bar, strategically position your chair so you won't be tempted.

Number 6: Being too honest

Okay, so you just got out of rehab, but there's no need to share this tidbit of information with your date (at least not if you want to see her again).

This is not to say that you should lie, but you don't have to tell her everything. That includes DUIs, divorces, speeding tickets, minor indictments, depression meds, the fact that you still live with Mom, or that case of syphilis from a couple of years back (which hopefully has cleared up). There may be a time to come clean, but it's definitely not on the first date. At least let her get to know you first before you start dropping truth bombs. Just remember: She probably has a few skeletons in her closet that she's not revealing just yet, too.

Number 5: Constantly interrupting

She mentions that she's been to England. You jump in to say that you've been there, too. She goes on to say that she loves Coldplay. You jump in again to say that you saw them live at Coachella and they were great. Well, stop right there and bite your tongue. Yes, shared interests are a must, but there's no need for you to keep interrupting her. Not only is it impolite, but it also tells her that you're more interested in hearing your own voice than hers. Instead, wait till she's done and then wow her with your similarities. Your politeness will be duly noted.

Number 4: Dressing inappropriately

Before stepping out the door on your big date, you give yourself the once-over. Your Derek Jeter jersey/ball cap/shorts/flip-flops combo (all clean and wrinkle-free) doesn't look too bad, if you do say so yourself. Well, think again. Unless you're taking her to a ball game, leave your sports jersey at home. Women put a lot of thought into their first date outfit—a lot. She probably even went out and bought a whole new ensemble for the occasion. And while she doesn't expect you to invest in new clothes, she does expect you not to underdress (see above outfit) or overdress (three-piece suit or tuxedo).

Number 3: Touching on taboo topics

Just in case you've been living under some rock (or have been out of the dating race for a while), the taboo topics for first date conversations are as follows: ex-girlfriends, past heartbreak, religion, politics, and money. This last one is especially important because, contrary to popular opinion, all women are not after your dough. In fact, yapping about it (in particular, how much you make and how much you have) could send your date running for the hills. Show her what you're worth; don't tell her about it. The same goes for name-dropping and bragging. Leave it for the locker room where it belongs.

Number 2: Staring at the waitress

It's not your fault the waitress is smokin' hot or wearing a V-neck down to her navel, but under no circumstance should you acknowledge this. No lingering leers, quick looks down her top, or flirting. None whatsoever. First of all, no matter how discreet you think you are, your date will notice. Second, women want to believe that you're with them because you want to be with them. Sure, they know that you'd opt for a Victoria's Secret model given the chance, but Gisele is just a fantasy girl. The waitress, however, is all too real. When you acknowledge her hotness right in front of your date's eyes, you're showing disrespect—a big no-no.

Number 1: Getting loaded

You want to have a good time, and, more important, you want to show her a good time, so what do you do? You order a couple rounds of tequila shots. Tequila equals fun, right? Wrong. This is not a bachelor party, it's a first date, and whether you like it or not, you're under strict observation. Having a couple glasses of wine with dinner is one thing, but getting drunk or plying her with alcohol is another—unless you want her to think you're still an immature frat boy.

Honorable Mention: Texting up a storm

Everyone knows that talking on cell phones is off limits (unless it's work-related, in which case, warn her in advance). Well, texting may not get as much airtime, but it's just as bad. It tells your date that she's not the most important person in the room (or in your mind), and shows her that you can't shut the world out for one measly date. If you start to go into withdrawal, you can try to sneak in a quickie while she's in the bathroom. Just make sure you don't get caught. That will make you seem sneaky and self-absorbed. To avoid temptation, your best bet is to ditch your device altogether. If you must bring it, leave it in the car. Out of sight, out of mind.

RECOVER FROM A BAD FIRST IMPRESSION

There are clearly a lot of first date taboos to be wary of. And we've only covered the general, most common ones—we haven't addressed those turnoffs that are unique to individual woman and can't be anticipated.

In light of this, initial blunders seem to be inevitable. So, what do you do if you unwittingly committed one of the dreaded first date faux pas? Is there a way to recover?

Mistakes will happen, no matter how tight your game is. It's tempting to think that all is lost if, upon initially meeting a woman or at the start of a first date, you somehow make a bad impression. Nothing could be further from the truth: it *is* possible to bounce back from a poor first impression or a first date blunder.

You come on too strong

Desperate and pushy are two traits that women regard as highly unattractive. Most guys don't try to come on too strong, but it is one of the more common mistakes we make. The fact is that being overly eager to get her number or convince her to meet you again easily translates into "I'm a desperate loser," thereby sinking all chances of a successful outcome.

If you notice that you are behaving in this way, you must act immediately. Stop pushing her, because it's only driving her away. Return to conducting a normal conversation for a few minutes, and be as funny and charming as you can without going out of your way to impress her.

You don't come on strong enough

Having a weak come-on is also disadvantageous to you. Let's say that you made a great first impression but didn't signal interest in her by asking for her number, or you didn't make plans for a second date. This behavior could lead to you being lumped into her "friend zone," or she could forget all about you and your otherwise solid first impression. She could even dismiss your belated advances as desperation.

The solution to this is easy and simply requires you to step up and be bold. For instance, if you run into her at the grocery store, casually ask her what she's doing for dinner, and if the situation presents itself, suggest cooking a meal for her later that week.

If you simply didn't call her, sincerity is your best bet. Call her up and apologize right away for misplacing the number. If you see her face-to-face, ask for the number again—and make sure you call.

You get busted looking at other chicks

Men constantly check out other women; we can't help it, and women don't like it. There's probably some evolutionary explanation for our behavior, and while that might hold water with geneticists, it won't cut it with the woman you're supposed to be impressing. Ogling other women paints you in a negative light and shows you up as being rude, untrustworthy, and likely to cheat or leave.

If she caught you mid-stare, don't ignore it or try to blubber your way out of the situation. A simple solution is to keep looking at the other woman (without a leery look on your face, obviously) and to claim some prior, loose acquaintance—you know her from a class, you're members at the same gym, or she's dating a work colleague—then quickly move onto the next topic.

"Fool me once, shame on you; fool me twice, shame on me." The loose-acquaintance ploy will probably only work once. Get busted again and you'll have to think fast. Pick up on a detail of the other woman's clothing and ask what it is because you think your sister would like it for her birthday. From that point on you'd better work on your self-control.

You talk about your ex-girlfriend

Talking about your ex-girlfriend is perhaps the worst thing that you can do. Doing so will create a terrible impression of you as a guy who is caught in the past, emotionally unavailable, a stalker, bitter, and blind to the beautiful woman you're talking with. The list is long, and none of it good.

The best solution is to drop the topic immediately and don't return to it. There's a danger that the girl may want to pursue this topic, but don't allow this to happen. Even if you're in the middle of a lengthy explanation of why you broke up, shrug it off with, "It didn't work out," and concentrate on the woman in front of you.

Steer the conversation to a better topic and repair all the damage by showing an appropriate, but definite, interest in her.

SECOND DATE SUCCESS

So you made it to the second date. Good job. You're relieved, you obviously made a good impression, and she wants to see you again, but now what? What is she expecting? And, more important, what could ruin the potentially good thing you have going on?

The girls' perspective

Of course, all girls are made different, inside and out, but there are universal standards that can guarantee success on your second date, no matter how unusual the girl you're after is.

AskMen.com talked to five different girls, all of them of different ages and with different life goals (yes, all of them are hot), to find the answers on what can make or break the success of a second date.

If you follow these three tips, along with the ABC cheat sheet tricks below, your second date will be a success—and you'll be gliding into the much-anticipated third date in no time.

1. Make her feel comfortable by . . .

A) Being yourself: just act natural

This is the most important rule of all. Usually when a second date is considered unsuccessful, it's because the guy wasn't being himself—he was trying too hard. So don't do or say anything that feels unnatural or forced. If you're comfortable, she'll be comfortable. The best thing to do is to keep in mind that if you lose this one, it's not the end of the world, so relax. Don't try to impress her; she'll see right through you. Just have fun with her.

Cheat sheet trick: A good trick is to pay attention to how you speak. You should sound natural and at ease with yourself. Avoid using clichéd lines like "Pick you up at 8?" Instead, stick with a more natural language. Call her up and say, "I'd like to come get you. Where are you gonna be later on?"

B) Getting rid of any awkward situations

You don't want her to associate you with any kind of awkwardness—on your part or on hers. Do whatever it takes to make your date free of uncomfortable situations so that the two of you can relax and enjoy each other.

Cheat sheet trick: Take charge and pick her up rather than meeting her somewhere and have her face the dreadful awkwardness of waiting in a strange place by herself.

C) K.I.S.S: Keep it simple, stupid

Don't do anything spectacular or you'll scare her off. Plan an activity that's different from the first date, but make sure it's nothing too demanding. The second date is about getting to know each other better. Have a few options planned, but don't force her to choose or she'll feel put on the spot.

Cheat sheet trick: Do something light and fun. Think of little destinations or missions the two of you could go on that are easy. For instance, go on a mission to get a specific brand of popsicle and walk in the park with them or go try homemade raspberry beer at a bar that makes their own brew. Make it an event, but a simple one. Your best bet is to make it casual and painless.

2. Make her feel she's interesting by . . .

A) Using your memory

A man's memory is the quickest way to a woman's heart. Show her you remember details she mentioned on your last date. This will win her over, guaranteed. Girls go crazy when a guy remembers things she said about herself.

Cheat sheet trick: If you remember a few details she told you about her life on the first date—how many siblings she has or a little story— and you bring them up again, you're gold in her books.

B) Asking more questions

Some of the most successful second dates were winners because the guy knew how to ask questions. Asking her lots of questions will make her feel special. But balance it out: You don't want to sound or feel forced.

And don't ask clichéd questions or you'll come off as anxious and desperate. You have to show interest and make your questions interesting at the same time.

Cheat sheet trick: To keep your questions sounding natural, a good trick is to look at her and ask her questions about one of her current attributes, like, "Where did you get that watch?" or, "So, how much time did it take you to grow your hair that long? Really? What was the shortest you ever had your hair?"

C) Looking into her eyes

Looking into a woman's eyes shows her that you have self-confidence and that you can be trusted. It will make her feel important, attractive, and it will get your pheromones going—hers, too.

Cheat sheet trick: When she's talking, don't get shifty. Look straight into her eyes. You'll see that it will get her excited because she'll feel that she has your full attention. If she gets shifty, you're being too intense. Remember: You don't want to look unnatural, so don't overdo it with the gazing.

3. Make her feel wanted, not needed, by . . .

A) Complimenting her on three different things

Compliments are tricky: It's all about balance. Make a conscious effort not to overdo the compliments. Make her feel wanted, but don't put yourself below her. Don't just make her feel lucky for having good qualities; make her feel lucky that her good qualities are appreciated by you. Do this by saying things like, "I think you are so much fun," instead of, "Wow. You are so much fun." Putting yourself into the compliment equation makes you look less desperate, which, in the long run, is more of a compliment for her.

Cheat sheet tip: Choose three different things you like about her, and give her a nice compliment on each throughout the date. Things you can think about are:

■ Her looks (hair, legs, eyes, smile)

■ Her style (clothes, shoes, bag)

■ Her taste (in music, food)

■ Her personality (intelligence, how fun she is, how easy she is to talk to)

Start your compliments with, "I think . . ." or "I find . . ."

B) Saying "I want . . ." vs. "Should we . . . ?"

Another sure way to a woman's heart is via the language you use. Make her feel wanted by starting sentences with "I want," and then including her in them. Remember: You must include her in the phrase or else you'll come across as selfish. Your goal is to make her feel good about herself and her relationship with you. Everyone wants to be wanted.

Cheat sheet tip: Say things like, "I want to have a drink with you" instead of "We should have a drink" or "Do you want to have a drink?" For example, instead of saying "I thought we might go here," say "I want to go here with you."

C) Showing her she's desired, not admired

You've got to be very careful to show her that you want her physically, but that you don't need to be with her. This way you'll look less desperate. Girls love a guy who's relaxed and not needy. Make your second date a fun exchange between two people. Expect a slight make-out session, but nothing too heavy. You're both hot for each other, but you're still feeling each other out.

Cheat sheet tip: Don't ask permission to kiss her—girls hate that. It puts her too high on a pedestal and it puts you way below her. Being at her feet won't make her feel sexy: She has to feel like she's scoring too, not like you're trying to score and it's up to her to decide if she wants you. Girls want to feel desired, not admired. Tell her you want to kiss her; tell her you think she has beautiful lips and then go for it.

She says: "Why don't you try to kiss me like this?"
She means: I don't like the way you do it.
Why she does this: She doesn't want to hurt your feelings. But this is not all bad; she likes you enough to want to work at it and make it better.
What you should do: Try it her way and see how it goes.

Ultimate rule: Don't bring a gift, just show her a good time

Don't bring flowers! Contrary to popular belief, many girls are uncomfortable receiving gifts, especially on the second date. Don't bring her anything. Instead of a gift, offer her a simple compliment, like "I've been looking forward to seeing you again," or "I think you look great."

Remember: Relax. Be yourself and make her feel comfortable. Keep it light, easy, and simple. Make her feel that she's wanted by you without coming across as desperate, and, most of all, make it fun, and you'll have a successful second date.

RULE 3
TRANSITION FROM FRIENDSHIP TO RELATIONSHIP

Not all courtships begin with a meeting of two strangers. The woman you have your eye on may be a longtime acquaintance: a friend or a work colleague. How do you transition such an established relationship into being a romantic one?

WHEN A GIRL FRIEND BECOMES A GIRLFRIEND

The word "friend" is rather broad in scope, but the addition of a prefix can change its entire meaning. The word "girlfriend" makes you think about anniversaries, dating, and sex, while "best friend" makes you think of fun, comfort, and a shoulder to lean on. Can the two be combined?

More than your best friend

Of course, your long-term girlfriend is likely to become your best friend, but what about when your best friend becomes your girlfriend? She has always been one of the guys, the girl you could hang out with even if you just crawled out of bed wearing a ripped, worn-out T-shirt (the one your ex-girlfriend always told you to throw out).

She complains to you about menstrual cramps and you don't cringe. You tell her openly about what you had to do the other night before bed after your date left abruptly without allowing the evening to progress fully, and she confesses that she had to do the same thing when her boyfriend had mono.

One night, you see her out, and she looks incredibly sexy, and you realize that you're unable to stop thinking about her. You begin to see her in a different light. That's it; you've fallen for your best friend—hook, line, and sinker. But is this relationship feasible?

Make it happen

You never thought this could happen and you can't understand how you even got to this point. The question remains: Could she possibly feel the same way about you? Should you reveal your feelings? That's probably unnecessary, since she can practically read your mind. She knows what it means when you're biting your nails and clenching your jaw—there's something important on your mind.

What could you do? Before approaching her to reveal your innermost feelings, you must assess your position. This is a very difficult, fragile situation, and there is no turning back once you tell her how you feel. You can't blame the alcohol when she laughs in your face and tells you that you must be kidding.

WEIGH THE CONSEQUENCES

A list of pros and cons must be assessed before venturing into this uncharted territory.

Pros

■ You like her personality: you already know she's smart, how her mood swings work, what makes her happy, and when to steer clear of her.

■ You get along and have a great time together; you have common interests, and even when there's nothing to say, you share comfortable silences.

■ You know her parents: this already knocks off one of the things that can be extremely nerve-wracking—meeting her family. You're so comfortable in her home that when you watch TV with her family, you can hold the remote control!

Cons

■ You know what she likes and how to please her. Although this could be a major bonus, the fact that you'd be skipping the intriguing part of discovery may breed boredom quickly.

■ You're taking a big risk; you have a lot to lose in the way of friendship. You can't imagine her not being a part of your life.

■ You may not be compatible in every area. Being best friends with someone doesn't mean you will be compatible intimately. Besides, you'd lose the person who anxiously listened to your complaints about loser dates. Who are you going to complain to about her?

As you can see, there are more pros than cons, but the cons carry more weight because they add up to the fact that you may lose a wonderful friendship. You may think you know everything about her, and perhaps you do as a friend, but when she becomes your girlfriend, everything changes.

Is it worth it?

While there are great risks involved in confessing, dishonesty may endanger the friendship if you behave awkwardly because of those newly discovered feelings. Bashing every guy she wants to date, or telling her you hate her wearing those tight little outfits out will not bring you two closer.

You may wind up being the best thing that ever happened to her. Don't ignore these feelings, because they may resurface if you try to sweep them under the carpet. Sit down, weigh the pros and cons, and remember that the risks involved could be worth it. You will never know what you could be missing out on if you don't consider giving it a try.

If the two of you are as close as you think, revealing your feelings may not cause more than temporary awkwardness if she doesn't have mutual feelings. The greatest relationships grow from great friendships. Maybe she'll even let you wear that worn-out raggedy T-shirt in public!

FRIEND TO FLAME IN 5 EASY STEPS

If you're looking to turn your good pal into something more than a friend, you'll have to change her perception of you. The following five strategies will help her see you differently. The tips are set out in the order in which they should be followed, but you won't necessarily need all of them to achieve your goal. Remember: You needn't be covert or sneaky about your efforts to court her—in fact, the steps below go from less to more suggestive. So if you've thought it through and are ready to attempt the transition from friend to flame, read on.

Disclaimer: Observe her reaction at each step to make sure she wants to go in the same direction you do. You may have to sacrifice the friendship if you make a move when she's not actually interested.

She says: "I think of you as a brother."

What she means: I'm not attracted to you.

Why she does this: She probably wants to preempt your hitting on her with this sneaky little line. It serves the purpose of letting you know she's not into you, and, of course, it's kinder than telling you the truth.

What you should do: In this case, it's what you shouldn't do: Don't make a move on her.

Step No. 1: Highlight the physical characteristics you possess that you know appeal to her.

Don't tell her outright that you have large biceps, pecs, or other body parts—this will come off as egotistical and very tacky. Instead, try to subtly accentuate these body parts or characteristics. And make sure you are well dressed and smell great each and every time you see her. In the past, you may have allowed her to see you all sweaty after the gym, but you now have to look impeccable every time you see her. No exceptions.

Step No. 2: Curb all "guy talk" in her presence.

In order to start the transition from friend to flame, you have to put an end to all guy talk when you're around her. That is, stop talking about other women you're dating or have dated in the past, and don't comment on other women in general. For her to consider changing her perception of you, you need to treat her like any other woman you're interested in, and not like "one of the guys."

Step No. 3: Place her in an environment that will enable a shift in her perception.

Rather than taking her to your usual hangouts, take her to a "date" environment like a trendy restaurant. Wherever you choose to take her, though, make sure that it's just the two of you. For your relationship to grow, you need to maximize alone time with her, so try to subtly suggest one-on-one activities without expressly telling her that's what you're doing. For an added touch, don't call her to ask her out at the last minute like you might do with a friend. Instead, invite her out a few days in advance.

Step No. 4: Act chivalrous.

Adopt polite "boyfriend" behavior whenever she's around: Open the door for her, pick her up and drive her home, start paying for meals and drinks, and so on. Your new chivalrous attitude will give her a taste of what you'd be like in a relationship—and with any luck, she'll like what she sees.

Step No. 5: Use suggestive body language.

Instead of telling her how you feel, try hinting at it with your body language. Make frequent eye contact, and gently touch her shoulder, back, and waist. Compliment her often so she knows you're paying attention. Start this kind of behavior subtly; if she responds well, move on to more suggestive behavior.

Make her fall for you

As you're going through the above steps, note her reaction. If she seems responsive to your overtures, then it's time to make your move. If, on the other hand, she is unresponsive or even pulls back (women are very intuitive, so she might be on to you), then take her hint and give it up. And what should you do if she exposes your efforts and throws them in your face? Admit defeat and confess. Tell her that while you have feelings for her, your friendship is still your top priority.

OFFICE ROMANCE: IS YOUR FEMALE CO-WORKER FLIRTING?

You've had your eye on this one lady in particular, but she's got you so confused that you're analyzing her moves more than the accounting reports your manager handed you this morning. However, moving from co-workers to a couple is an even more perilous transition than going from best friends to bed mates, because it could put your career in jeopardy.

This is not a nightclub where you can make your move, risk rejection, and move on to the next cute honey. Oh no, the stakes are much higher, and rejection might be there to kick you in the face every time you see her at the photocopier thereafter.

You also don't have your buddies to back you up; this is something you'll want to keep to yourself, unless you want your crush to become part of an office memo. Before you go straight to the source and proclaim your love to the female co-worker of your desire, check out our guide and consider it the most important document at the office ... if you want to maintain your pride and your job, that is.

Let's get physical

You have already learned the effectiveness of body language. Even if you always express your feelings through verbal signs, you could be reading into others' signals completely falsely, and seeing only what you want to see.

Because the power of body language accounts for the majority of human communication, observers must make sure their eyes are not deceiving them, and that the woman in the cubicle across the way really is signaling come hither.

Her hair

Is she playing with her hair while you're around or while you're talking to each other? Whether she's constantly pulling it back in a ponytail, twirling it around her index finger, or flipping it from side to side with her hand, her mannerisms could be telling you to play with her hair.

Giveaway: she's slowly running her fingers through her locks.

Her face

Observe how she reacts when you tell her certain things about yourself. Does she smile the whole time you're conversing? She might look down and completely avoid eye contact altogether (she's nervous and timid), or maybe she thrives on eye contact and keeps her eyes locked on yours the whole time you're chatting away (she might want to make contact).

One trick is to watch her reaction if and when she finds out you're not seeing somebody, for example. Did she all of a sudden look shy or become quieter? Or did she suddenly let a smile creep up on her face when she found out you're as single as a one-dollar bill?

Giveaway: she's touching or licking her lips.

Her body

Next, you'll need to check out her body—do this subtly, and it will be worthwhile. Does she stand in an inviting manner, or does she seem to shut herself off from you? Does she fidget a lot? Playing with her nails and twirling her foot inside her Prada pump are signs that she's pleasantly nervous about talking with you.

She doesn't need to be a walking disaster in order to show interest; the general idea is to watch out for the subtle signals she's giving you for free. If she looks nervous or bashful, or talks to you in a cheerful, inviting manner, it's possible that she has her eye on you.

Giveaway: she uses her hands when she talks, and does so in an inward motion, pointing toward her body.

Her touch

There are always those women who'll touch you while you're talking. She might put her hand on your shoulder while she's telling you something important, place her hand on your back when she's laughing because you just cracked a great joke, or even touch your waist to tell you that there's something wrong with the printer.

Giveaway: during conversations, she will put her hands lightly on your arm, shoulder, or back.

Here's the clincher: Observe how she acts and reacts with other men at the office. Some women are just affectionate and touchy with both men and women (all right!), and you shouldn't mistake her hands-on behavior for a business proposal.

Time for your orals

In order to really know if your co-worker is flirting or not, it's best to combine her body language with what she says to you, and how she acts toward you overall.

On a professional basis . . .

There could be flirting signals where you least expected.

She singles out your reports

If she's your superior and she always uses you as the perfect example during morning meetings, you can rejoice in the fact that she thinks of you as an exemplary employee. But if you're both equals and work on the same team, and she refers to your reports in particular, she could be sending out a sign and hoping you'll take notice.

She takes detours

You're noticing more and more that she makes a point of passing by your desk, no matter where she's going. Say your workstation is the one closest to the water cooler; is she filling up her glass ten times a day, and then passing you again on her way to the ladies' room? Either she's interested or she always eats Mexican food for lunch.

You develop an e-mail relationship

E-mail can be very deceiving, but it can also be a great flirting tool, since you're likely to write things you wouldn't say in person. However, it is a double-edged sword, as it can be misleading, especially if you read her cute emoticons as declarations of affection.

On the social front . . .

You take breaks together

Work breaks can be a great way to bond with co-workers, even if it's for a short period of time. Getting a cup of coffee together can even become a ritual, but you'll have to distinguish between friendliness and flirting.

If she always makes an effort to come get you for coffee or a fresh-air break, or e-mails you to announce that it's break time, she could be making an effort to spend more time with you. This is especially true when it becomes a ritual, to the point that you feel you have to apologize if you can't go because you have a deadline to meet.

You go for lunch together

The same goes for lunch breaks. If she initiates going for lunch together often—even if it consists of sitting at the office together, eating and chatting—then it is possible that she's flirting.

But be careful: If your lunch breaks become replacements for actual dates, she could just be looking for another friend.

You get together after work

Again, if she asks you to go to the local happy hour after work, there's a big chance that she wants to get to know you better . . . unless she wants to chat about how to deal with her insecure boyfriend.

She stays with you at the Christmas party

Observe how she acts around you at corporate social affairs, such as the much-anticipated Christmas party or fundraising gala. If she insists on standing by your side at the party, and pulls you onto the dance floor whenever a slow song or one that requires maximum body contact is played, it can safely be taken as flirting.

If you both show up alone (and the invitation was for two), and she asks you where your date is, she probably has a personal motivation for doing so.

She pays you compliments

This can be her way of being friendly. If she always singles you out and pays you compliments on everything from your good hair day to your nice shoes, then she could be looking for ways to talk to you.

She inquires about your personal life

This can also be perceived as a way to make small talk, so the context in which she asks makes a difference. Are you out for lunch when she's grasping for icebreakers, or is this during the workday, when you won't necessarily have time to chat about it?

Watch, learn, and think

Women can be very confusing (that's no newsflash), and to make the distinction between her sincere efforts to make you feel comfortable, her drive to become Miss Congeniality at the office, and her penchant for teasing every guy in the office, you'll have to observe how she acts with other employees, both male and female.

If you don't really have a chance to watch her since she works at the other end of the office, you can make a comment to a colleague at work, like "Mary is really friendly," or "Mary and I are going for a drink after work," just to see the other guy's reaction. If he says, "Yes, Mary really is a sweet and friendly girl," you've probably got yourself a woman who wants to be sociable at work. But if he finds it odd that Mary is making such an effort with you, or he doesn't even know who Mary is, perhaps her friendliness is directed toward you and you alone.

If you do make a comment to a colleague, never say anything incriminating or negative about another co-worker; that kind of office gossip can come back to haunt you.

And if you do establish that this female colleague is in fact trying to get cozy with you, make sure you know the repercussions of interoffice romance. Dating a co-worker is never a good idea if you work in a small office, or if the female co-worker is your superior or subordinate.

But if she works in an entirely different department, or, better yet, a different floor, then you might have a chance. Before you do anything, read up on the company's rules and regulations about office dating.

Sure, the woman of your dreams could be giving you all the right signals, but if you care about your job, it's probably not a risk worth taking. If she moves to another company or either of you gets laid off, well, then, that's a whole other story.

FLIRTING VS. TRUE ATTRACTION

It's not only female friends and colleagues who will send confusing signals. You will find yourself in plenty of situations where being able to distinguish between harmless flirting and true attraction will spare you from embarrassment.

When men and women spend a lot of time around one another, flirting becomes a means of communication and entertainment that can make everyday interactions more fun and exciting. Just like other interpersonal activities, though, each person flirts and accepts flirtation differently.

While some people flirt constantly, others reserve this affectionate type of interaction for expressing genuine feelings that extend beyond friendship.

Either way, it can sometimes seem impossible to tell whether flirtation is just for fun or whether it's an invitation to take things to the next level. If there are true feelings behind the flirting, it's important to be able to recognize them in order to avoid any awkward or destructive situations. Sometimes a flicker of the eye or a brush on the arm can reveal volumes about the underlying relationship. Read on for tips on how to read her flirtatious activities and figure out if her interest extends beyond playfulness.

Level of attention

Flirtation that's simply flirtation will tend to be flippant and fun. Friends who don't harbor a real attraction for one another will play, and then move on to the next thing. They have nothing invested because there are no feelings involved. If a gesture or a touch is prolonged, however, it could mean that she's trying to get your attention to push things beyond the status quo. When flirtation is exaggerated like this, it could also mean she's enjoying it so much that she doesn't want to let you slip away, which is also an indication that there's something else behind it. There is a fine defining line between these two levels of play, and people tend to differ on what they expect of flirtation, but you'll likely notice if somebody gives you this extra bit of attention.

Exclusivity

Some women are just flirty. If she's scooting around giving everybody in the vicinity a wink and a nudge, there's likely nothing special in the look she throws your way. In other words, if she uses casual flirting to throw a twist into an otherwise boring day, there's probably nothing more behind it. If, on the other hand, she pays special attention to you, there's a good chance you've been singled out for a reason. If it's not in her nature to flirt with just anybody, she may be trying to communicate how she really feels about you. Used like this, flirtation is a way to feel you out before she puts herself on the line.

Intensity

The key to friendly flirtation is lightheartedness and subtlety. Two people who flirt often will likely have a rhythm to their interactions; it's like a routine. This type of play has underlying and unspoken boundaries that maintain a friendly feel. If her flirting suddenly becomes more intense, however, it could indicate deeper feelings.

For example, during your regular banter about relationships, she might start singling you out as the ideal man. Or she might start surpassing your regular physical boundaries by putting her hand on your leg or your hand when she's sitting beside you. If her actions become more serious or obvious, you may have an admirer on your hands.

Eye contact

Eye language is a very important indicator of the feelings between two individuals. Think of how you interact with your friends, male or female. Eye contact is often made during face-to-face conversation, but it is casual and frequently broken over the course of the exchange. If she makes prolonged and sustained eye contact, on the other hand, it could mean that something beyond friendship is afoot. Another indicator is if she mirrors your body language while you talk, extending the sense of closeness you both feel.

These types of actions—whether they're performed consciously or not—could mean that she's trying to catch your eye in a romantic sense.

Duration

Flirtation is fun and entertaining, but if it isn't serious, it usually passes with time. Because there are no true feelings wrapped up in the friendly sort of flirting, a "love 'em and leave 'em" rule tends to govern these actions. On the other hand, if the two of you have been flirting consistently for an extended period of time and it's not waning, it's possible that there are deeper feelings behind it.

Think back on how your relationship has evolved. Is she still seeking you out after you've moved to new flirting grounds? If so, it's likely that she's trying to linger in this type of activity until she can get her real feelings of attraction across. Not only can this indicate existing feelings of interest, but prolonged flirtation with a single person can also lead to them, so tread carefully in both instances.

Intimacy

Flirting involves a broad range of activities, from conversation and mockery to gestures and touch. These actions can either be playful or they can extend to a more personal level. If flirtation began at—or has progressed to—a more intimate level than most friendships, you can take a hint that there's probably more to it.

For instance, conversation between friends can get flirty, but if she tells you personal things or asks you questions that reach a more emotional level, she's probing beyond the scope of friendship, and it's likely that she's interested in pursuing a relationship. Likewise, if you go beyond an arm brush to holding hands or hugging, you have reached the next emotional level.

Whether flirting is just friendly or it hides other feelings, it's important to recognize its true nature. If the romance is one-sided or inappropriate, it's a good idea to shut down the flirtation before it becomes difficult to deal with.

She says: "I don't want to ruin our friendship."

She means: I am not attracted to you, or I don't feel enough chemistry to date you—but I do like you as friend.

Why she does this: She probably does want to remain friends, but doesn't want to hurt your feelings by admitting that she doesn't feel the same attraction for you.

What you should do: Don't take it personally; she just doesn't feel the same chemistry as you do. Take the hint and work on being friends with her, if that's what you want.

RULE 4
SAIL THROUGH THE COURTING PHASE

t only takes a few dates to transition from making a woman's acquaintance to finding oneself in the midst of a developing relationship. Of course, the work doesn't end here; if anything, increasing levels of intimacy and the move toward exclusivity make managing an emerging romance all the more complicated.

The courting process is largely a pleasurable one; it offers the joys of discovering another person, revealing yourself to her, and having great sex together. Courting also carries with it some negative points, however: anxiety over her feelings, initial clashes of opinion, and plenty of cash spent. In light of this, it's worth making sure that your prize really is a woman worth pursuing, not a loser or a lunatic. Here are some signs to help you determine that.

TOP 10 SIGNS SHE'S MADE FOR YOU

All of your life, you have been the single guy. You have never been able to envision yourself settling down, let alone trusting women, but suddenly you meet this gift from heaven and she makes you wonder what could have possibly hit you across the head. So how do you know she's heaven-sent? Here are the top ten signs she's made for you.

10. You trust her

You have had difficulty with trusting women your whole life. Then, one day, you realize that you can trust the woman standing beside you. For the first time in your life, you don't think twice about opening up about personal matters or letting her take care of important objects; you know that you can turn your back to her and not worry. You even want to introduce her to your friends and family.

9. She gets along with your friends

She meets your friends one by one, and you get the eerie impression that she likes them and could actually get along with them. Better yet, she understands and encourages you to spend time with them and have your own life.

8. She has fun with your crazy family

You cringe at the thought of her meeting Grandpa Joe and hearing his sordid tales . . . but when the big day comes, you realize that she actually finds his stories funny. She seems to care for your parents, and she likes your siblings.

7. You forget your friends

You always chose hanging out with the boys first and the girlfriend second, only now, playing pool and having some drinks with your buds just isn't as interesting as it used to be. You prefer to see her and pass up the friends.

6. You forget about your ex

You've been thinking about the ex-girlfriend for some time now, until you meet this new goddess. From the time you first laid eyes on her, you seem to have finally turned a new page.

5. You get mad when others disrespect her

Whether it's your friends, family, or some stranger, you get irritated when people say mean things about your woman. You contemplate smashing their skulls, but opt to make them eat their words instead.

4. Chemical balance

You have so much chemistry oozing between the two of you that you have no choice but to give into temptation. She is on your mind at all times, and every time you go shopping alone you end up buying her something. You can stare at each other for hours and not say anything; you have achieved "the comfortable silence."

3. You ask yourself where she has been all your life

She wants to know all about you—the good and the bad—and she isn't turned off by the latter. You envision yourself married to her and wonder what your kids would look like. While this thought would have made you nauseous years ago, it now brings a smile to your face.

2. You treat her

Your idea of cooking may have been delivery or microwave meals, but suddenly you'd love to fix up a five-course meal for her, serve her, wine and dine her, and then take her in your arms. You were once a cheapskate, but you now spend all your discretionary income on her. You even clean your pad when you know she's coming over.

1. You find yourself unable to concentrate

Being productive at work has become increasingly difficult, listening attentively in class is a daunting task, and all you can think about is when you will see her next. As pathetic as it may be, you cannot wait to see her again, and you even consider calling her to let her know just that.

9 SIGNS YOU'RE DATING A LOSER

En route to finding that one winner, you're likely to encounter plenty of losers. And while you can usually spot them a mile off, it's easy to get caught up in the excitement and ignore the facts, you want it to work out, so wrap yourself in the warm blanket of denial. Well, it's time to wake up! There are more losers and crazies out there than you might expect. Are you dating one?

No one should ever settle for mediocrity, yet so often the women we date either hold us back, bring us down, or simply hurt us in one way or another down the road, in every sense of the word. Gentlemen, if any of these signs are all too familiar, then head for the hills and leave home without her.

9. She has freaky friends

You look forward to meeting her friends, but your interest level fades as you realize that they are not the coolest of people (cool is used here in the "have a pulse" sense). And guys, it is not the quantity of friends that makes someone cool; it's the quality and level of trust, admiration, and camaraderie among them. If you sense any mistrust, jealousy, or envy in her inner circle, bolt.

8. Jealousy is her middle name

You have no problem admitting that another dude is good-looking and that her friend Bob is funny, yet she has a nervous breakdown when you tastefully mention that a certain woman has nice features, great style, or a good sense of humor. She is quick to jump to conclusions because "men are this way and that way . . ." Are we? Well if we are, go get yourself another one.

7. She has no life

You insist that you should have your own lives, your own friends, your own dreams and aspirations, yet you should still share a common bond. This girl wants to be your Siamese twin. Before you know it, she sticks to you like glue and puts a trace on you. Break the silence and let her know that you will not stand for such a sentence.

6. You are her goal

Any woman who only has "finding a man" on her list of aspirations will drain you and lead you to an early grave. Yes, men like faithful women, but we do not need someone who lives and breathes us. Granted, the less confident, controlling, and possessive men may need someone like that, but not the quality men. If you like such women, you should ask yourself some serious questions, and if you are with such a woman, change this path right now.

5. You're her first

There is nothing wrong with being a single woman, but only if being single is by choice and not for some other mysterious reasons. If you realize that you are the woman's first love interest ever, then you may have to ask yourself some questions.

4. She sees everything and everyone as competition

You would think that she is confident enough about your affection for her, but she cannot stand you being with your friends, talking to other women, or even occasionally putting your job ahead of her. Despite your giving her the world, she seems to doubt and question your true feelings and always brings up frustrating "issues."

3. She blames you for her exes

Yes, some men are bad and some have committed sins. But the same way that thou shalt not blame the son for his father's sins, men should not get blamed for other men's mistakes. Blaming, distrusting, and attacking you for others' mistakes is a recipe for disaster.

2. She has no respect

Whether she has no respect for you, your friends, your parents, or herself, it's clear that this woman has some severe issues. Some guys get turned on by the idea of improving a woman's life, but no one can save or rescue anyone else, and if she has no respect for herself, then it is a lost cause. Sink her and move on.

1. Her sense of humor is nonexistent

No sense of humor and no sense of objectivity: no potential for a future.

TOP 10 SIGNS SHE'S CRAZY

Is the girl you're dating acting a little crazy? The first few months of seeing a woman is something of an introductory period, over the course of which you get to know her and find out if she's nuts. It's best to take full advantage of this grace period, before you get yourself mired in a committed relationship with someone who should be committed.

Some signs that she's crazy can be obvious, such as if she lives in a cult compound, a jail, or a mental hospital. In all seriousness, more often than not, the signs are less obvious.

For the purposes of dating, a crazy girl can be defined as one whose behavior is out of the norm, who scares you, or who poses a physical danger to you. Read on for the top ten signs that she's a nutcase you should drop like a bad habit.

Number 10: She calls you endlessly

She's constantly checking up on you to find what you're doing, whom you're with, how your day is going, and so on. The telephone seems to be her monitoring device, a way of knowing where you are at all times. And if you happen to not answer one of her calls, she'll keep hounding you until you pick up, and then she'll drill you about not answering. This is more than just annoying; it leads you to question her behavior and underlying mental state.

Number 9: She's been in weird relationships

As you get to know a girl, she'll likely open up to you about her past. When she does, listen to find out what kind of guys she's dated. Keep an ear out for a history of emotionally or physically abusive relationships. Does she claim that her ten past boyfriends all had clinical problems, or that, coincidentally, they all got restraining orders against her? Pick up on her past relationship experiences to find out what they say about her.

Number 8: She hijacks your family and friends

She's infiltrated your circle of family and friends like an intelligence operative. Maybe she goes shopping with your sister, or regularly talks to your mom on the phone. She might even go to the movies with your best friend's girlfriend. And while all this might be innocent in and of itself, the problem is that you don't even know that she's doing it. It seems that her motivation is to find out more about you, or to build alliances with your friends and family. And the end result is that it will be harder to dump her because she'll have your loved ones in her pocket.

Number 7: She argues in public

It's normal for couples to have disagreements, but she instigates confrontation . . . in public, no less. She'll accuse you of one thing, then she'll scream at you because of another. Whatever the reason, it's never the time or place for her outbursts. Furthermore, she nitpicks and criticizes you in front of your friends and family.

Number 6: She's unpredictable

You can never anticipate her behavior or what sort of mood she'll be in. She has wild mood swings, breaking down and crying spontaneously or screaming over petty things for no apparent reason. She might even be clinically bipolar. In any case, she's a loose cannon, one who could become violent and physically attack you or hurt herself. You should consider these signs before making her part of your life.

Number 5: She lies constantly

She lies to you compulsively about everything and anything, big or small, and does so for no reason. She might fib about going to a movie, when she really went to have a coffee with her girlfriend. She might not necessarily be trying to hide something, which is what makes the lies so strange. If you observe her consistently lying to friends, family, and co-workers, there's no reason to think that she isn't lying to you, too. You might have a pathological head case on your hands.

Number 4: She interrogates you

In her eyes, you can do no right. So, she likes to play detective and find out what mischief you've been up to. She wants to know why you were ten minutes late meeting her. Or she demands the details of the discussion you had while you were hanging out with a buddy. Your answers will never be enough. She always wants to know more; she must know anything and everything that involves you.

Number 3: She snoops around

It starts with an invasion of your privacy, and then, to make matters worse, she confronts you about whatever it is she thinks she discovered. Maybe it's restricted to casual glances around your apartment for clues of other women in your life. Or it could go as far as to involve thorough searches of your living and work spaces, including the monitoring of e-mail or voice messages without your knowledge.

Number 2: She freaks out over other women

They could be hot, or not, but she freaks out regardless. Whether it's with an elbow nudge or a discreet (or not-so-discreet) pinch of your arm, she's going to let you know that you shouldn't be looking. The really scary thing is that you may not even be looking in the first place. This sort of illogical, all-consuming jealousy is an example of serious insecurity.

Number 1: She stalks you

She follows you around to "check up" on you. You might have told her that you were going for a few beers with your buddies at the local bar, only to have her show up unannounced. The worst part is that she thinks this is normal behavior! If she calls and e-mails you incessantly, and shows up at your home or office unexpectedly, you might be in need of a restraining order.

Don't jump to conclusions when you first witness one of these signs. If multiple ones appear, however, then you need to ask yourself whether or not you really want to get into a relationship with this woman.

If she is crazy, it's sad, but it's not your problem. You aren't her therapist. So, get rid of her before she drives you crazy and let some other poor chump deal with her.

TOP 10 TRAITS OF A GREAT BOYFRIEND

As you discreetly monitor her behavior in an effort to gauge whether she's a winner or a wacko, remember: The romantic evaluation process is a two-way street. She is looking at you just as keenly as you are at her, seeking out the signs that you're a keeper.

With that, here are 10 positive traits of attached men. And if you possess just about all of the following, then perhaps the problems in the relationship don't lie with you.

Number 10

You listen. When words come out of her mouth, do you actually pay attention to what is being said, or does your brain just process mumbling sounds while you stare at her chest? A good boyfriend is an active listener, meaning he asks questions and doesn't just sit there waiting for his turn to speak.

Showing her that you have a genuine interest in what she has to say means, among other things, that you respect her opinions and find her interesting.

Number 9

A great relationship is one that never feels stale. To keep your flames of desire burning, always keep her guessing. If you remain unpredictable and mysterious, you'll keep her on her toes.

Whether you whisk her away to a Mexican resort at the last minute or show up, for no apparent reason, with Chinese takeout, wine, and a pair of handcuffs, spontaneity can add some real excitement to the romance, and intrigue her all the more. Women love to be swept away in as many different ways as possible; it's up to you to come up with as many ideas as you can.

Number 8

Saying that sex is important would be a gross understatement. A good boyfriend must satisfy his woman's every romantic need (and yes, she should reciprocate). There's a difference between making love just for the sake of it, and being passionate about it. That means never skipping fore-play, sending her soothing messages during the act, and not falling asleep the minute you're done.

Number 7

She may feel more empowered by it in the beginning, but in the long run, no woman wants a passive, submissive man who completely com-promises his personality to make her happy. Retain your personality, stand by your opinions, and don't give in too easily. Show her that you are strong, confident, and have a spine.

Number 6

Did she suddenly get highlights in her hair, shed a few pounds, or buy a new dress? These are all things you need to take note of; most women instinctively gravitate to guys with keen eyes. It shows that you are at-tentive and don't skim over life's more subtle details.

Number 5

You give her space. Trust is the foundation of any good relationship. Part of that entails giving her the freedom to have a life separate from yours without asking twenty questions or having jealous fits, and knowing that she's not taking your trust for granted. Keep things in perspective; would you like a girlfriend who kept tabs on every move you made? Probably not, and the same goes for her. And always look for a silver lining; in this case, you'll have time to hang out with your buddies, and have something to talk to her about the next time you see her.

Number 4

You respect her (and her family). It's important to avoid letting your ego get the best of you, so if your mentality is stuck in the '50s, you must adjust to changing times. You have to understand that she's an equal part of the relationship, so appreciate her company. Likewise, try to embrace her family early on. In addition to scoring precious points, being kind and courteous toward her parents is a good way to show that you're serious about the relationship. This includes, but is not limited to, bringing the parents thoughtful little gifts every so often, and planning activities that include her whole family, like a picnic. Of course, this is assuming that you've already survived that dreaded first meeting. For more information on this, see Rule 8.

Number 3

You better yourself. Demonstrating what a positive effect your woman has had on you is a fantastic way to gain leverage. Whether you're getting yourself back into shape, improving your vocabulary, or forgetting about the television long enough to take dance lessons with her, it doesn't matter. Improving yourself is a great way to let her know she deserves the best, and she'll be flattered that she was the inspiration behind your desire to aim higher.

Number 2

You challenge her to be better. Likewise, your role in her life should be just as beneficial. You should inspire her to make changes that reflect the positive effect you've had on her. If, for example, you see her letting a great talent go to waste, encourage her; maybe that's all she needs. Don't be afraid to sign her up for an art class, or push her to pursue a career you know she'd be good at. The fact that you care that much about her well-being will make her want to keep you around longer.

Number 1

You make her feel beautiful. Reminding her how beautiful she is comes with making her feel good, and makes you a poster boyfriend. Best of all: Simplicity and honesty are all you need. Buy her, say, a card that expresses your appreciation, compliment her at odd times, and if you feel that she's the most gorgeous creature you've ever laid eyes on, be sure to let her know. Women want to look good for their men, and proving to her that you only have eyes for her will be a validation of that.

Keep each other happy

It all boils down to making her feel good about herself and appreciating her in an unselfish way; find success in this department, and she will love you eternally. More important, however, if all of the above describes you perfectly and she still takes issue with the little things, then maybe it's time for you to reevaluate how good a partner she really is for you.

8 WAYS TO MAKE HER SWOON

Aside from having cash and good looks, there are many things a man can do to make a woman flip for him. Many men feel as though they need to be puppy dogs to make women happy—this is not the case. It is possible for you to maintain your identity and your masculinity but still make your girl feel on top of the world. If you've just met a woman or are new to a relationship that you'd like to pursue, these tips will have her spinning and falling right into your arms.

1. Go the extra mile

If you really want to impress her, do more than she expects. Women tend to have very high standards for themselves, but lower ones for other people—especially for men. If you think ahead and outdo her expectations, she'll be thrilled and consider you her knight in shining armor. Every now and again, go out of your way for her in a big way. It's good to talk regularly; sometimes it's better to call unexpectedly because you miss her. If you're supposed to pick up dinner, get her a small gift "just because." You get the idea.

2. Talk her up

When you're around other people, the couple dynamic is often lost in the crowd. You both end up talking to different people, and it's easy for either one of you to feel a bit deserted. If you're around her friends and family, the best way to bring the dynamic back is to let them know how great she is.

Tell them how consistently she's been working out, how organized she is, or how well she does at work. They probably already know, but they'll love to hear that you're taking notice. Women don't like to hear that their friend is with an unappreciative guy, and this will let them know you recognize exactly what you have. It will also make the two of you feel closer because you'll be remembering all the things you like about her and she'll feel fantastic about hearing you say them aloud.

3. Show her you're smitten with her

For women, there is nothing as irresistible as being irresistible. Since men are not exactly known for wearing their hearts on their sleeves, women often have little indication of how things are going. This is one reason that being aloof doesn't always bring the best results—contrary to popular belief. If you show her how you feel, she'll feel special and wanted, and in turn, she's likely to feel the same way about you.

There are many ways to show your feelings, and they don't necessarily have to include anything too mushy or feminine. Just be eager to see her, let her know if you were looking forward to a date or really enjoyed a previous one, and if you really like her, tell her you want your friends to meet her. Making her feel wanted is half the battle in making her keen on you—it's really that simple.

4. Include her in your life

It's not necessary to have a girl around all the time in order to keep her in your life. It may sometimes seem like it, but you don't have to give up boys' nights and *Monday Night Football* in order to make her happy. You should, however, ensure that she's involved in some of the more important elements of your life.

As previously mentioned, an introduction to your boys can mean the world to her, even if it's just on a Tuesday pub night after work. If there's something major going on in your life, confide in her. Even if you're not ready to invite her along to your family Christmas dinner, a description of what it's like might make her feel as though she's in the loop. Also, show interest in her life, job, and friends—this is equally important in the process of making her feel crazy for you.

5. Be original

When relationships are new, they tend to follow a pattern of expected behaviors. Deviate from the plan: Think of something interesting to do, introduce her to new music, or talk about new things. This way you will leave your mark on her. Most women have met men before you, and most women are not with those other men for a reason. If you show her what sets you apart from the others, she'll more likely be interested in finding out more about you. She'll find these new things exciting, and she'll feel as though her life is enriched by the fact that you are around. Wrap her up in new things, and she may just find you irresistible.

6. Have a sense of humor

This includes two things: making her laugh, and being able to laugh at yourself. Now, the first one does *not* mean telling blonde jokes during dinner. Rather, be relaxed and have fun without trying too hard; wit is priceless in the dating world. The second area—being able to laugh at yourself—will always be a simple, but priceless, guide to good humor. There's nothing worse than a person who takes himself too seriously. If you slop on your shirt at dinner, don't get stressed out and swear up a storm. Recognize your foibles and accept them. You'll be much happier, and you'll put her at ease.

7. Reassure her

As discussed, this isn't a newsflash, but women like to be complimented. This isn't purely due to vanity on her part; it's more about her need to know exactly where she stands in life and in her relationships. This is why women so often run around cooing at one another about looking great, losing weight, or their fabulous accomplishments. Since women like to hear it, they indulge their fellow femmes with all the reassurance one could possibly stand.

Likewise, if you tell her that she looks great or that you continue to be pleasantly surprised by how ultimately cool she is, she will also get a confidence booster and feel more appreciative of you for saying so. In particular, if you know she's feeling insecure about something, be sure to allay her fears. She's surely deserving of the upcoming promotion, for instance, because she's such a capable and hardworking employee. You'll be her hero, and that will pay dividends in the end.

8. Be a good listener

Although this is widely promoted as a key feature that women seek out in men, it is rarely explained properly. As a result, many men don't know whether or not they're the fabled "great listener." Being a good listener involves really caring about what comes out of her mouth and responding with questions or thoughtful comments—but only when it's appropriate.

If she's telling you about a feud with her mother (which probably doesn't top your list of interests), you don't have to stick to the subject all night, but you should hear her main concerns and say the appropriate sympathetic things. It is not likely advisable, however, to give her advice on her dealings with her mother. Rather, just let her know you feel bad that she feels bad. A few minutes spent consoling her will likely stick favorably in her mind.

ANNOYING BEHAVIORS: 7 THINGS MEN THINK WOMEN LIKE

In the midst of trying to be a good boyfriend, you may find that some of your attempts to make her swoon are actually making her nauseous. Unfortunately, we men are often misguided as to the kind of behavior we think women like; thus, our actions don't always yield the results we hope for.

The following are seven things that men think women like—and that you might be surprised to find out they actually don't. So read on to find out which relationship sins you've been committing. You may find that once you curb these annoying little behaviors, your results in the dating arena will soar.

Now wouldn't that be worth a little self-reflection?

1. You try to spend all your time with her

Why it will work against you: She'll obviously want to partake in some activities with you, but if you consistently insist on spending all your time with her, you will seem needy and dependent, and she'll just feel smothered by you.

What to do instead: She'll likely want you to share enough hobbies and activities that you can spend time together and enjoy each other's company. But don't invite yourself to activities that are decisively hers, like her girls' night out or her book club meeting. And this works both ways: Unless she is interested in sports, you don't have to drag her to a game, either.

2. You try to help out around the house but leave a mess

Why it will work against you: Sometimes your well-meaning favor might not actually be so helpful. For example, when you cook her dinner, do you leave pots in the sink for her to clean? When you repair the sink, do you leave gunk and dirt on the floor? If your so-called favor is not actually helping her in the long run, she'll end up resenting it.

What to do instead: If you want to help her around the house—or anywhere, for that matter—make sure you are really helping. You're better off cooking dinner only once in a while—and doing it properly—than leaving a mess for her afterward.

3. You share all your feelings too soon

Why it will work against you: Women generally like a man who is in touch with his feelings, but sometimes this can be taken to the extreme. Droning on about past relationships, work dilemmas, or family troubles can make you seem whiny and too emotional—a real turnoff.

What to do instead: You need to strike a balance: Share what you're thinking without complaining or giving away too much too soon. A good way to gauge this is to evaluate how much she shares with you; if she hasn't told you her entire life story, then you can wait a little bit to tell her yours.

4. You are too honest

Why it will work against you: Too much honesty can be unnecessary and sometimes hurtful. If you tell her you're not so hot on her cooking, for example, the only thing you'll achieve is making her feel bad about herself and, consequently, about you.

What to do instead: Listen up, because this is important: Total honesty is a must for big things like infidelity, financial issues, and family matters. However, when it comes to small things—like "Do you like this outfit?" or "Do you find that woman pretty?"—sometimes it's okay to tell a little white lie. In fact, if being brutally honest might make your woman feel bad about herself, whereas telling a little lie wouldn't really hurt her in any way, it's probably best to go with the fib.

5. You insist on paying for everything

Why it will work against you: Chivalry is great, but to a degree. A woman might want to pay her own way if she is unsure about the relationship or if she doesn't want to feel like she owes you something afterward. Therefore, insisting too strongly might actually backfire and make her feel uncomfortable.

What to do instead: You should offer to pay, especially when you first start dating. And you can even insist—but no more than twice. Watch her reaction and be wary of making her feel uncomfortable. If you see she really wants to pay, go dutch and leave it at that.

6. You join her in her shower or bath

Why it will work against you: She probably enjoys this most of the time. But consider this: Has she had a bad day at work? Is she not feeling well? If so, your sexual advances might be more of a nuisance to her than anything else.

What to do instead: A woman will often take a bath or a shower to relax and take her mind off things, so try to judge her mood and what she wants in each instance. Don't automatically assume that her bath is a sexual invitation. Keep in mind that there may be times when she needs her privacy.

7. You're never serious

Why it will work against you: If you tend to continuously tell jokes when you're nervous in an effort to fill the awkward silences, you may be annoying her just as much as if you didn't have a sense of humor. In fact, too many jokes will just make her think you are avoiding a real conversation and simply being a clown.

What to do instead: Try to judge her reaction to your jokes. Does she appear to genuinely enjoy them? And even if she does, don't forget to intersperse your jokes with actual conversation. Be prepared to ask her questions and listen to the answers.

What women really want

Don't feel bad if you've been regularly committing any of the above woman-repelling behaviors; it can be hard to weed through the dating lingo and figure out what women really want. But after reading this, you should be ready to purge yourself of these nasty little dating sins.

WOMEN'S TESTS AND HOW TO PASS THEM

The positive and negative cues described thus far are those that women will keep an eye out for over the early weeks and months of a relationship (if not longer). Her other evaluation strategies, however, will be confined to single events, "tests" that she will throw your way in an effort to extract information about your personality via your reaction. She still wants to see if you're the man she wants, and here's your chance to prove that you are, by passing all her tests.

Now, she won't always give you an indication that one of these tests is around the corner; that's why you must stay on your toes. And if you think this just means not adjusting your crotch in front of her or not letting unwanted air pass from any orifice while she's around, then you need to read on to see what she's really looking out for.

This is only a test

The family test

If you've listened to her attentively, then there's nothing to worry about. Remember that first date when you discussed each other's family lives? Well, here's your chance to put your listening skills to the test. If you remember things about her family, mention them while on later dates with her, by asking her whatever happened to her sister's sick dog, or referring to something she told you about her father's golf game. If you don't remember what she told you, or don't even know whether or not she told you, just ask her; you'll score points by showing a sincere interest.

She says: "Do you get along well with your mother?"

She means: Are you a family man?

Why she does this: A man who gets along with his mother tends to be more loyal, sensitive, and devoted—at least that's the stereotype that a lot of women buy into.

What you should do: Talk about how close you and your mother are; you could even tell a couple of stories. Just enough to affirm that yes, you get along with her.

The gift test

Once you're at the "just like that" gift-giving phase, you'll learn why it's the thought that counts. She says she loves Chinese philosophy; you buy her *The Tao of Pooh*. She says she looks forward to that time of day when she can just kick up her feet in the bath; you buy her an oil burner that she can use while she's bathing. These little gifts don't need to be big, but they will speak volumes about your thoughtfulness and attention to detail.

The door test

When you take her out on the first few dates, it's a given that you'll walk her to the door when you drop her off—you knew that, right? But just because you're past date number five, it doesn't mean it's all downhill from now on. If you don't walk her to her door when dropping her off, always wait for her to get in the door safely before driving away. Never speed off while she's left there fumbling for her keys, even if Game Seven of the World Series is tied and you want to catch the ninth inning. You'll strike out.

The waiter test

You treat her with respect, but is that the real you or the "you" that wants to butter her up? She wants to know how you will act with her friends and everyday people you encounter, and she'll know how you treat others by watching how you interact with total strangers. Do you thank the waiter when he brings you a glass of water, or do you throw the water on his face when your order is messed up? How you treat others—especially strangers—is a reflection of how personable and down-to-earth you are.

She says: "Do you really want to go to that restaurant/movie/dinner party?"
She means: I really don't want to go to.

Why she does this: She doesn't want to go, but she doesn't want to appear stubborn either. She is probably hoping you'll sense her hesitation and come up with an alternate plan that pleases her.

What you should do: If you have your heart set on going to that particular destination, stick to your guns—you don't want to get into the habit of rolling over for her. Otherwise, you might want to switch up in order to please her.

Remember this: If you keep her happy, she'll keep you happy.

The "Is she prettier than me?" test

This one is the trickiest, and pretty near inevitable. She will set you up for this one, and the less you say, the better off you'll be. It can happen anywhere: You could be walking down the street or watching a movie; you could even be sitting in your living room together enjoying a cocktail.

She'll ask you about a friend of hers, a famous actress, or a woman walking down the street. Always say something like: "Why do you even have to ask me? Don't you know you're the prettiest?" or "Don't you know no other woman compares to you?" This will probably come your way once you're dating steadily. Just give in.

She says: "You have a knack for dealing with kids. They really seem to respond to you."

She means: I am contemplating eventually having children with you and am wondering where you stand in that department.

Why she does this: An indirect question is her way of feeling you out without freaking you out.

What you should do: Don't freak out. She is probably thinking very distantly into the future (yes, women do this). If, however, you absolutely positively know that you never want kids, this would be a good time to say it.

The "I had a bad day" test

She comes home from work wanting to rip someone's head off, and it looks like you're the victim. She phones to complain to you about what a horrible day she had at the office, and she's close to tears. Do you run over to comfort her, or do you go out with your friends as planned, assuming she'll be fine once she watches her favorite TV show?

You don't have to go over to her place to cheer her up, but it definitely wouldn't hurt. While you're talking to her on the phone, ask about her day, and if you don't already have plans, ask whether she wants you to come over and have a night of pure vegging. If you already have plans, then it's up to you whether or not you want to break them. If you can't break them, tell her how sorry you are that you already made plans, and if you can, stop by her house on your way out just to hold her close in your arms for a few minutes, stroke her hair and her face, and reassure her that she'll feel better in the morning. Bonus: Bring along her favorite ice cream.

How would you fare?

The aforementioned scenarios and your reactions to them prove that while it's tempting to fall into a comfort zone with your girlfriend, you should still be making an effort to show her that you're the guy for her.

These tests are smaller parts of the "deeper meaning" exam, which prove to her that you're compassionate with others, pay attention to detail, respect her, and can be spontaneous when it counts. There's no need to break a sweat because if you know her, then you'll know exactly how to act in order to please her—and, in the long run, to please yourself.

ARE HIGH MAINTENANCE WOMEN WORTH IT?

All women give tests, but if you feel like your new relationship is like a marathon exam session, then there's a chance you're dating a high maintenance woman. High maintenance women are like high maintenance sports cars. They're lots of fun when you're out on the town together, but for every hour of showing off, there are another ten spent on upkeep and repair behind the scenes. After hours of polishing the headlights in your garage, you might ask yourself—is this really worth it, just for a couple of rides? Read on to learn how to identify these demanding gals, and the positives and negatives that go along with them.

Telltale signs

Broadly defined, high maintenance women are those who need many things (money, material goods, affection) to be happy. These women love dressing up whenever possible, and are obsessed with all aspects of their personal appearance and grooming. This almost obsessive attention to detail usually extends beyond their person, to their homes or apartments, their pets, and yes, even their men. In addition, they tend to be perfectionists, overachievers, self-centered, and a bit vain.

Need a quick litmus test to determine whether she's high maintenance or not?

Ask yourself the following questions: Do you let her pick out her own gifts on her birthday and at Christmas because she's so picky that you don't want to bother giving her something she'll only return anyway? Does she often send back food in restaurants if it's not exactly to her liking? Does she put makeup on whenever she goes out, even if it's just to the grocery store?

If the answer to any or all of these questions is yes, then you are definitely dating a high maintenance woman. Fortunately, there are some upsides to this situation.

Pro: She looks like a million bucks

High maintenance gals are arm candy, pure and simple. Their fascination with their own looks means that whenever they step out of the house, they look perfect. And guess what? When you're with someone who looks good, you look good too. It's not just self-aggrandizement, either; there's no shame in feeling proud of being with the foxiest woman in the room at a party. She puts great effort into looking great, so when it pays off, more power to her! And to you.

Con: She knows she looks like a million bucks

The worst pitfall to dating this type of woman is, without a doubt, dealing with her vanity. She's never met a mirror she didn't like, and even if her looks aren't her absolute highest priority, they're still near the top of the list. Constantly discussing the minutiae of her appearance ("Yeah, the red skirt is cuter . . . Can we go now?") is just plain tedious.

And other negative traits accompany vanity, such as being a spendthrift; she may blow huge wads on things like manicures, tanning, and keeping up with each and every trend. She may also take herself too seriously and not be able to withstand even the gentlest teasing about her personal appearance or quirks. Who wants a woman with no sense of humor about herself?

Pro: She's a source of free style advice

This type of woman likes to be with a man who can match her when it comes to looks and status. She never dates "down," if you will. She will encourage you to buy, or will even buy for you on her own initiative, things that she thinks will better your appearance. She will give you constant advice on grooming, whether it's about haircuts, which styles suit you, or what the heck you should do with that facial hair. Left to their own devices, men often end up looking like slobs or get stuck in a style rut and never leave it. However, if you're dating a high maintenance woman, she'll make it her mission to make you as put-together as she is.

Con: Free style advice = nagging

Occasional well-intentioned advice can be helpful. Constant nagging about perceived flaws in one's appearance, on the other hand, is extremely irritating. The downside of dating a fashion maven is dealing with her critical nature. Maybe you like those old jeans you've had since college, even if they are getting a little ratty. Why should you stop wearing them just because she turns her nose up every time she sees you in them?

Pro: She's a challenge

For men who like to be challenged on a daily basis, the high maintenance girl is the perfect choice. She likes attention, compliments, and fancy dinners, and she demands the best of all these things. She will keep you on your toes, refusing any response from you other than absolute respect.

Honesty tends to go hand in hand with this woman. She's usually a straight shooter who's eager to let you know when she's not pleased, which can be very refreshing for a change. You will always know where you stand with her because she makes her needs clear.

Con: She can't be satisfied

On the flip side, the high maintenance woman is like a ravenous beast, always wanting more of everything. She will find faults in all your best efforts, and honestly, some women just aren't worth the bother.

Pro: She's sugar and spice and everything nice

High maintenance often translates into a pleasant femininity in straight women. They're not rough-and-ready, they can be a little dependent, but they're also appreciative when you do nice things for them. Men who like "girly girls" tend to go for this type. At first, it's cute if she relies on you to squash a spider for her or open a jar of pickles. Many men enjoy playing the part of caretaker, which is the role they are usually directed into when in the company of this type of woman. If you like feeling needed and useful, this is the perfect woman for you.

Con: She has Princess Syndrome

Just like all the other cons, this one is simply the previous positive point taken to an unhealthy extreme. Über-feminine women are often victims of what can be called "Princess Syndrome," or excessively precious behavior stemming from the belief that they are somehow above certain tasks. Some high maintenance women may just flatly refuse to shoulder their share of the load. For example, she's the type of woman who always makes her husband do all of the yard work and mowing because she is too "delicate" for it. Typically, they hate camping, hiking, loud parties, and more. In other words, if you're looking for an equal partnership, do not date these women.

If you can take the heat

For a certain type of man, high maintenance women are well worth the time and effort of wooing and winning. If reading the above caused a tingle in your spine—of fear, that is, not desire—then you're not one of them. Cut and run, because at the end of the day, if the woman in your life is more of a bummer than a booster, she's just not worth it.

DEALING WITH HIGH MAINTENANCE WOMEN

High maintenance women, divas, princesses . . . if you've come to the realization that your new partner is a demanding one, you certainly have your work on your hands. And while the task of taming a high maintenance girlfriend can be daunting, it can also be very rewarding. They can change, evolving into kinder, more caring people over time. All it takes is a little patience and ingenuity on your part. By employing the strategies outlined below, you can successfully defuse a diva.

1. The preemptive strike

The number one rule in dealing with high maintenance women is simply this: From day one, do not accept any disrespect. This can't be emphasized enough; if you allow her to run roughshod over your dignity with her pointy little stilettos even once, you'd better believe it will happen again and again. Curb the diva's thoughtless actions right away.

For example, maybe you've just started dating and you notice that not only do you always pay for dinner, but she has come to expect it, and never shows any gratitude. Don't lose your temper or argue about it. Instead, one proper technique would be to nonchalantly take her out to a low-end restaurant or fast food joint one night. When she responds negatively to this, don't bat an eyelash; just let her know that if you always have to foot the bill, it's not going to be the Ritz every night.

High maintenance women love to provoke their men but don't get drawn into their imaginary crises. If she calls you freaking out about an offense you've committed and you know that her beef is absolutely unfounded, don't react similarly. Coolly tell her that you'll talk to her once she's calmed down and is reasonable again—and hang up the phone. That should put an end to her game.

2. Strategic targeting

We've discussed the importance of nipping bitchiness in the bud, but does this mean that a guy should always be on "diva alert," armed and ready for attack? Of course not. The name of the game is picking one's battles. Know the difference between small, everyday disagreements and unnecessary aggression, and respond accordingly.

Take the following scenario: If a woman often complains about one of your obnoxious friends, and he truly is obnoxious, it's probably not worth the fight. Let it slide.

But if she's picking on a good friend with little reason, stop her immediately. Arrange for him to drop by when she's at your place and initiate a friendly conversation between them. If he's being genuinely nice, she'll have to admit it and drop most of her complaints about him. Under these circumstances, if she still finds fault with him, she's clearly being unreasonable and is in the wrong, and will have to acknowledge as much.

3. Sudden strike

It's also important to remember that when you do decide to combat her behavior, you must do so with maximum force. Be firm, but never resort to using her brand of dramatics. For example, if she's pushing you to spend every waking minute with her, and you've already warned her nicely several times that you need a little more space, the "sudden strike" method would be to just flatly tell her that you're spending the whole weekend apart, and then follow through. Those few days apart will help her come to the healthy realization that she is not the center of your universe. As a result, she'll be less demanding and happier to spend time with you in the future.

Here's another example: Maybe she's constantly late and you're sick of it. Stop the cycle with a tough response. If you're at her apartment waiting for her for the gazillionth time while she's primping, tell her that she's being inconsiderate, and just leave.

If she doesn't show at a restaurant or elsewhere you were scheduled to meet, don't put up with it. Call her and calmly tell her that you didn't have all night to wait for her, so you left. It's that simple.

4. Operation: hearts and minds

Make love, not war. Sometimes a princess's attitude can be adjusted more quickly with kindness than with opposition. Wield sweet words like weapons; they're even more powerful. If your diva keeps making catty remarks about a pretty woman at the party, a good way to turn the conversation around would be to say something like: "Some women have to dress that way to attract attention. Not everyone is as naturally beautiful as you are."

This strategy shouldn't be overused or you'll risk reinforcing her diva-ness. Occasional use is most effective; respond to her snarkiness with the correct ratio of kindness and confidence. Compliments are a bullet to the heart for most women.

5. Abort mission

Kenny Rogers put it best when he sang, "Know when to hold 'em, know when to fold 'em, know when to walk away, know when to run." In some rare situations, you may come across incurable divas whose poor conduct doesn't even change slightly with time, regardless of your persistence.

These high maintenance monsters can be recognized if they do any or all of the following: They show no remorse, they refuse to apologize for their screwups, they never show an interest in your life, or they complain constantly. Look for bad behavior patterns, and if you see no progress in curbing her wicked ways within a few weeks, throw in the towel. This woman is unworthy of your time and energy—no matter how hot she is.

BECOMING EXCLUSIVE

You've established that your new woman is someone that you want to spend more time with, so you begin to do just that. And the more hours you put in together, the more you both might start to wonder what the future holds. After the nerve-racking dating and courting stages, the next big step in any relationship is deciding whether to become an exclusive couple. And no matter how you feel about the subject, it helps to know what she may be thinking, so that you can navigate these treacherous waters with skill.

What goes through a woman's mind when she decides that she wants to be exclusive with you? It's a multistage process.

1. Curiosity

She's curious to know more about you and wonders what you will do next—that is, if you provide enough mystery.

2. Enjoyment

She enjoys the time the two of you spend together. She likes spending time with you. She enjoys you.

3. Hesitation

She wonders how you feel about her and where the two of you stand.

4. Desire

She longs to see you again.

5. Self-Doubt

She wonders whether you're the one for her, whether she should still see other people, and what she wants out of relationships in general.

6. Excitement

She's anxious for the two of you to have "the talk."

7. Fulfillment

She's fulfilled by your presence only and doesn't want other guys. And she hopes that's how you feel, too.

She says: "Where is this relationship going?"

She means: I would like us to graduate to a more serious, exclusive relationship.

Why she does this: She wants you to be the one to suggest exclusivity.

What you should do: This depends on whether or not you actually want exclusivity. If so, suggest it. If not, let her know that you care about her, but are not interested in being exclusive right now.

Making the move

Sure, it's fun to start dating, but it always seems like that interim period—the transition from dating to exclusivity—is the most insecure. You're not sure whether you should be dating other women at the same time; you're not sure if you should be mad at her if she dates other men; and you don't know whether you can call her at the end of the day, for no reason at all but to say "hello." Yet, this is an exciting time, one that makes you most nervous, most uncertain, but can turn out to be very rewarding.

Going from dating to exclusivity should be a natural transition, one that gradually occurs from dating to becoming an official couple. It no longer involves the "Do you want to be my girlfriend?" question that made things so easy for you in high school.

How do you do it?

So what's the best way to go about it, and how do you know you and your girl are an exclusive item? Simple. When you know that you share the same feelings. When you know you can call each other at the end of the day. When you know you can ask her to be your date for a corporate party. And when you know you can just spend a Saturday night together, order in, and watch the James Bond marathon on TV.

You may need to have the talk, but it should just be a discussion that clarifies where you stand, so that you know you're on the same wavelength, and she won't be planning to go on that blind date with her friend's co-worker next week. You can go about it by saying something jokingly, like, "So, who did you pick up at the nightclub the other night?" or "What do you tell your friends about us?" It can be done casually and is just a way to seal the deal, so to speak, to ensure that you're on the same page.

And once the two of you have decided that this is where you want to be, that's when the real drama begins. If you want an encore presentation, then you'd better make sure you play the part well.

LEAVING THE PAST BEHIND

Do you find yourself inexplicably reluctant to agree to exclusivity? Is everything going well, but you are still holding back? Whether are you finding it difficult to commit to a new relationship or you are even finding it difficult to open up and let her see the real you, the problem could be baggage from your previous relationship.

You have recently met a woman who seems perfect: fun to hang out with, attractive, intelligent, a good conversationalist, and she gets along with all your friends. You're on your way to a new relationship. There is only one problem—can you trust her? Your heart has been blown to bits more than once, and it took you so long to recover from your last girlfriend, your friends were buying you self-help books. You want to be able to move on to a new level with her, but you are still suffering from the wounds you received in your last relationship.

How can you move into a new and healthy relationship with all the baggage you're still carrying from your past? Can you succeed in letting go of the past and moving on with a new girlfriend after you've been burned so many times? Learn where you can store your luggage in order to move on with a new woman.

Moving on

Although we learn from the past, it influences our future by making us wary of taking risks. Most of us have had our share of bad experiences, and have sworn that we would never get hurt again. Women rip up photographs of their boyfriends when their men upset them. Remember that picture the two of you took on your one-year anniversary? That's right—the half where you once stood is now at the bottom of her trashcan. You don't need to be told that men and women react differently to heartache, but one thing will never change: the vow that it will never happen again.

No one can undermine the pain and frustration felt when a lover breaks your heart. Heartache is the worst and shouldn't be bestowed upon even your worst enemy. While getting back into the game of dating and relationships after a relationship ends seems frightening, it also serves the purpose of helping you get your mind off the past. But the past never seems to leave for good, and will often creep up from the woodwork once you decide to become close with someone new. Do you really want to give all the women who have hurt you the satisfaction of tainting your love life for good? Absolutely not! So what can you do?

Excess baggage

The first thing you must realize is that if you have baggage, the potential woman in your life must have a load of her own. In fact, women probably have even more baggage than men, since women often seem to dwell on the past and are usually more emotional than men. If you have emotions that are bottled up and harbor resentment toward the opposite sex, women have probably already tried to think up ways to create a third sex to date.

Standing guard

The men who are sweet and open are usually the ones who have not been burned before. They are ready to open up to their partner, be honest with their feelings, and don't see the risks in expressing their emotions. When a man has been burned in the past, he is too scared to wear his heart on his sleeve, lest he let his guard down and become vulnerable by expressing his emotions to his new partner.

What can you do?

Be wary of generalizations. Remember that if you have been hurt in the past by a woman (or more than one), you probably feel that all your trust in women has gone down the toilet along with the cologne she bought you. One woman hurt you, and now you've branded the rest of the female population as heartless, conniving, and manipulative. Don't assume that every woman is a vixen who wants to rip your heart out and stomp all over it. Both genders possess some bad apples. The new girl you date is in a no-win situation, and she hasn't even done anything wrong. You're no longer the only victim of what your ex has caused; the next person you date suffers from your ex's actions, as do you. You will never trust the next person, by default, and that person is getting the raw end of the deal because some other woman has temporarily ruined your life.

Having been hurt in the past opens your eyes to women who have the potential to hurt you again. Be wary of these women, but do not jump to conclusions if you do happen to see the warning signs. By helping you recognize that it is possible to get hurt and knowing how to avoid this, the women who have hurt you have almost done you a favor. Now you are fully armed.

Naïve thinking, such as, "I'm too strong to ever get hurt," can only get you into trouble. Remember that the lesson to be learned is not that it is dangerous to be sweet and honest, but that you have to learn from your mistakes.

That being said, the worst thing that you can possibly do is become too afraid and too macho to act naturally in a new relationship. Everyone has some sort of baggage, but it's up to us to put our pasts aside and move on. If we don't, we'll all fall victim to a vicious cycle in which one person is hurt and refuses to trust the next, while this person will, in turn, make the other person not trust him.

We may have been hurt in the past, but the past can also be remembered for its happy moments. That's the kind of baggage you should take with you on your next trip to a new relationship.

TOP 10 NEW RELATIONSHIP DON'TS

The beginning of a new relationship is often the most electric and dizzying time; all you can think about is the awesome woman in your life. Although it may feel like you can do no wrong during those first few months of being together, there are some things you have to avoid like the plague.

Certain topics are very delicate at this point, and if you come on too strong, your girlfriend may take it as a warning sign that you're looking too far ahead. Go with the flow, live in the moment, and take a look at the following tips to help your relationship move along swimmingly.

Number 10

While physical attraction was probably what gave you the courage (or motivation) to initiate a conversation with your woman in the first place, it is important that you show her that sex need not come first. If you want to make this relationship a serious one, don't think of sex as a top priority. This is a great move on your part, as you are showing her how smitten you are with her mind.

Be patient, establish the strong bond you are yearning for, and the rest will fall into place. Holding off on what your libido is telling you will eventually pay off in spades.

Number 9

One small but important habit that needs to be broken is introducing your new woman as your girlfriend. In doing this, you might come off as insecure, making sure everybody knows you have a girlfriend. You're much better off simply saying, "This is Mary" to your friends—they'll understand the nature of your relationship by the public displays of affection you shower her with, and by the little mannerisms couples seem to exhibit.

Don't tell everyone you're dating; instead, simply imply it. She'll be impressed by the way you show her off without putting her on display.

Number 8

It is quite easy to slip into a comfort zone, and to settle into a "couple's routine," but the worst thing a man can do is take his girlfriend for granted. Treating her as a long-time wife in a dull marriage is not the way to go. If this is already happening, then you have contributed to your own downfall, as she is probably feeling unwanted and unappreciated.

No good can come from making her feel like baggage and letting yourself naïvely think she'll always be there for you. Remember how lucky you are to be with such a woman, and tell her things that will make her feel special.

Number 7

Although a serious commitment is what you want, there is no need to pressure her early on. Saying, "I love you" prematurely is a big no-no, as your girlfriend might feel forced to respond or may even reject you on the spot. Any talk of the future, like laying out plans for marriage and kids, can scare a woman off more quickly than your rampant back hair.

Show your affection by reaching for her hand as you walk in the mall, touching her arm as you converse across the dinner table, and making eye contact when she is talking to you. Don't feel that you have to display your newfound love right away—at the beginning of a relationship, it's all about taking things slow.

Number 6

It is imperative not to get into a pattern of buying your way into her heart. You may have purchased a tasteful gift in the early stages of dating, but now that you both feel there is a future together, it's time to stop taking out the plastic every time you see some nice jewelry.

You're actually wasting your money, spending it irresponsibly on her instead of saving up for something extremely significant—like your future. If you make sound decisions about what to get her at opportune times, the presents will mean more to her and will leave less of a dent in your bank account. Refrain from showering her with presents early on so that she doesn't get used to the "princess" treatment.

Number 5

It is true that you should be yourself around your girlfriend, but remember to hold off on displaying different facets of your personality until the right time. If you're a great cook, knowledgeable art lover, and a handyman around the house, don't let her know of your skills all at once.

One by one, when the need arises, reveal the things you know she'll love about you. In doing so, you compound her already growing love for you and offer fresh qualities for her to appreciate. By showing off too much initially, you leave little to liven up the relationship later on.

Number 4

Taking a new girlfriend to a family gathering the first few months into dating can often be misconstrued as too serious a move. Although you love your parents and quirky Uncle Bob, it is best to introduce your family at a time when she'll easily understand your motives and be able to put up with some uncomfortable questions from a rude grandfather.

Early on, her feelers are busy enough trying to establish if you are "the one"; throwing family into the mix is simply too much too soon. Of course, don't shy away from mentioning your love for them and the fact that your mother will adore her, but leave it at that until the time is right.

Number 3

You might feel the need to always pour on the charm in her presence, but this is actually the wrong vibe to emit. Sooner or later, she'll realize the phoniness of your actions—your girlfriend wants *you*, not an actor. By being "super romantic man" all the time, the originality and shock value that special nights should provide will be nonexistent.

Once in a while, surprising her with a candlelit dinner or some flowers will score big points, but pick your situations carefully and spread them out. Let her know that you do in fact have a romantic side, but tone it down and let little daily actions bear more importance than big productions.

Number 2

The last thing you want to do at the beginning of a budding relationship is put her down. More than any other time, it is in the first stages that you should be open-minded and accepting of her ways and habits. That is not to say that you should constantly give her a piece of your mind once you've settled in with her. It's important to keep in mind that you are walking on thin ice the first couple of months, and if you judge her immediately and frequently, she'll be out the door in no time.

Hold your tongue, be understanding, and be careful with your words so as not to hurt her. If you feel a strong need to express your opinion, make your comment a mere suggestion and not an insult. Instead of "That dress is ugly," say, "I preferred the beautiful black one you wore on New Year's Eve."

Number 1

A fundamental quality that is essential in any flourishing relationship is honesty. Telling lies or omitting pertinent things about yourself (like "forgetting" to tell her you love partying full tilt every Saturday night) will only lead to problems later on. Laying your habits—and everything else that makes you tick—out on the table is the only way to start a relationship you hope will last a long time.

Of course, sometimes little white lies cannot be avoided, but remember the bottom line: Don't lie about important things. No good can come from saying you come from a rich family when in fact you don't, or claiming you're a subdued intellectual when, in fact, you prefer beer and football to talking about Tolstoy.

THE THREE-MONTH MARK: SIGNS OF LOVE

You've dropped off the baggage from your previous relationship, battled past early relationship blunders, and have arrived at the pivotal Three-Month Mark. Of course, three months is a generalization. Every relationship develops at its own pace, but if you have passed the whirlwind of the initial meeting and falling for each other and find yourself on the cusp of a serious relationship—you are at the Mark, whether it took you two months or six to get there.

Many relationships start off in the same manner: the man and the woman cling to every word the other utters, every breath they take, and every move they make. All is peachy in the prelude to every serious relationship, but how do we know if the couple will make it past the honeymoon stage or if you'll just be her Three-Month Man? How do you know if this woman is right for you? Will she tell you she cares, will she show you she cares, or will she only tell others she wants you in her life?

I love you for the moment

There never seems to be any bad news in fresh relationships. New couples agree on everything from the kind of entrée to order in a restaurant to the amount of butter to put on their popcorn at the movies. Unfortunately, couples eventually grow out of the simple smiles of agreement and lively displays of affection.

There comes a time when the popular three little words are uttered and uncontainable feelings are bared. As already discussed, saying "I love you," however, is not necessarily the right direction in which to travel. That infamous little phrase is to be kept on reserve for the appropriate time. It is not a statement that should be tossed around like rice at a wedding.

Saying that you sincerely care about your significant other is worth much more than falsely claiming to love her. Lying to her might also jeopardize a potentially good relationship. This rule applies to both men and women, since partners sometimes feel the urge to amplify their feelings by projecting their affections onto the other. This is not to say that certain couples will never love each other; they simply shouldn't get caught up in certain moments of happiness and blurt out things that they may not ultimately mean.

She says: "I feel so close to you right now. You know me so well."

She means: I am starting to feel the L-word, but I don't want to be the first to say it.

Why she does this: It's a scary thing to be the first to say, "I love you." It's much easier for her to hint and hope that you'll take the plunge first.

What you should do: Do not—under any circumstances—say the L-word if you don't mean it. If you do feel it, then go ahead; otherwise, don't say anything. In the long run, you'll be happy not to get entangled in such a lie.

Show her the goods

As they say, "actions speak louder than words," and this is especially true for relationships. We become so accustomed to hearing the same old thing over and over again that in order for the words to make any impact at all, they must be backed up with significant actions. So, the next time you tell your lady that she's precious to you, don't forget to show her how you feel.

You don't have to buy her diamond earrings to do so. Why not just give her a massage or take her somewhere she has always wanted to go? It's so simple to tell a woman that she means the world to you, but is it just as easy to prove? How many of us, at this moment in our relationships, tell our ladies that we'd do anything for them, and then turn around and go drinking with our buddies instead of staying home with them on a Friday night?

A girlfriend will greatly appreciate the fact that you will forego an entertaining night of scantily clad women and booze to spend time with her when she needs you by her side. A relationship is like any other enterprise; it requires a great deal of time, effort, and devotion. Couples come and go, but real relationships are those in which the couple can survive whatever life throws at them together and come out closer than before.

RULE 5
INTEGRATE INTO EACH OTHER'S LIVES

You established that your woman was worthy of pursuit, and pursue her you did—successfully. You passed all of her tests, and she passed all of yours, and it looks like smooth sailing ahead. Before you get too comfy, however, keep in mind that there are more than two people involved in most relationships. The more serious the two of you get, the more likely your respective friends are to play a role in your partnership—and not always a positive one. Let's look at some strategies for managing the friends that both of you will bring to the relationship.

DEFUSE HER HATEFUL FRIENDS

A woman's friends have a huge influence on how she will perceive you, so it's crucial that you stay on their good side. Most of her girlfriends will give you a fair shot, but if you're unlucky, you may stumble upon a friend who has it in for you.

So what do you do when you are dealing with a hateful friend? The first thing you need to do is evaluate the situation: Are you treating your woman well? Does this hateful friend of hers have a legitimate beef with you? If her concern about you is legitimate, then you have to change your behavior in order to change her opinion of you.

But if you are on your best behavior and this friend of hers still hates you, then it's time for action. Below are six sneaky—but effective—strategies for defusing her hateful friend. These tactics are surefire ways to soften her up and get her to be on your side.

Sparkle in her presence

A woman usually confides to her girlfriends about the negative aspects of her relationship. If her friend hears overwhelmingly bad stuff about you, then you need to counteract this by coming across as a good guy every time she's around. Be in your best form—be upbeat and humorous around all of her friends and make sure you're not in a bad mood before hanging out with them. But be careful not to suck up—this will only make you appear desperate for approval and untrustworthy.

Look for ways to bond with her

Get her to see you for the nice guy you are by starting a project with her that will allow you to spend time together. This works especially well if the project involves doing something special for your girlfriend. Organize a surprise party for your woman and enlist the help of her friend. You can also get tipsy with her and ask for some insider's advice on your girlfriend. Hopefully, this will help to break down her guard and give the two of you a chance to become friends. But be careful not to appear as though you are hitting on her during any of these bonding sessions, since that will only have the opposite effect on your relationship.

Listen to her when she talks

You don't want to give her the impression that you are tolerating her only for the sake of your girlfriend (even if that's the case). The best way to achieve this is by engaging in a genuine conversation with her. Make an effort to remember details about her and bring them up in later conversations. This will show that you sincerely want to form a friendship with her—and she'll notice.

Be chivalrous

When you go to open the door or to take your girlfriend's coat, don't forget to do the same for her friend. Being a gentleman is a simple, low-effort way to get her friend on your side. Always make sure to give a little more attention to your girlfriend and don't go overboard with chivalry if it's really not in your personality—it will look forced, and both your girl and her hateful friend will see right through it.

Demonstrate your affections in front of her

Let her hateful friend see you treat your woman with affection. This doesn't mean that you should slobber all over her or perform other unsightly PDAs in front of her friend, but do make it apparent that you care for your special girl by giving her compliments or by putting your arm around her. Your girlfriend's friend wants her to be loved and appreciated. If she sees you giving your girlfriend extra attention, she'll think good things about you. Let her hateful friend see you treat your girlfriend the way she deserves to be treated, and she'll have no reason to disapprove of you.

Perform a boyfriend-type task for her

You want your girl's hateful friend to think that you are a dependable guy. Helping her out with a "boyfriend-type" task is a good way of letting her know that both she and your woman can depend on you. Help her move, fix her car, or install her air conditioner, but don't make it seem like you are doing it to gain her approval. Let her benefit from your manly know-how, but make sure you let everyone know that you are doing these favors because you love your girlfriend or you might end up with a jealousy problem.

If all else fails . . .

If you've tried all of the above tactics and you're still getting the hate vibe from your girlfriend's friend, there is no better way to handle the situation than with a head-to-head tactic. There are two ways to do this:

1. Discuss your concern with your woman

If her hateful friend is starting to cause problems between you and your girl, it's time to speak up. Have a conversation about it with your girlfriend in a calm and gentle manner to let her know that you are concerned that her friend is not giving you a fair shot despite your genuine efforts. Be careful to avoid any trash talk about her friend. This will make your woman feel like she has to choose—and she may choose her friend.

2. Address the issue head-on with the hateful friend

If you see that her beef with you is irrational and none of the above tactics have been successful, you might have to address the issue directly with the hateful friend. Sit down with her and calmly explain that you have been trying your best to have a friendly relationship with her, but you don't feel she is responding. You can also mention that it would be in your girlfriend's best interest for the two of you to make an effort to like each other, since you are both important to her.

Can't we all just get along?

If you implement the above tactics, use some social skills, and have a little luck, not only will her hateful friend soften up toward you, but she may even become your biggest fan. And remember this: If her friends like you, your woman will care for you even more.

THE WOMAN WITH MANY MALE FRIENDS

Sometimes, conflicts over friendships can emerge for the simple reason that the friends are of the wrong gender. Most guys are unable to ignore the twinge of jealousy when their girlfriends choose to spend time with other men, even if they are supposedly "just friends."

As her boyfriend, you should be one of her closest friends—if not the closest—but that doesn't mean you should be her only male friend. Men typically feel threatened when they're dating a woman with a slew of men friends, but there might not be anything to worry about at all.

How many is too many guy friends, anyway? Five? How about five times as many as your weekend baseball team? It's hard to quantify what constitutes an exaggerated number of male friends, since it's relative to her circle of friends; as a rough guide, one could say that if more than 60% of her friends are male, that can be considered a lot of friendly testosterone.

If that's the case, then you need to know what you're getting yourself into and not act surprised when she mentions all her guy friends.

Who is this so-called friend?

You've established that your new honey has many guys calling her to simply "hang out"; it's up to you to figure out why she has more males surrounding her than Miss June in a photo shoot. It may be because:

■ she was a tomboy growing up;

■ her female friends turned on her;

■ she's more interested in sports than hair and makeup;

■ she was raised in a family consisting of more boys than girls.

Although the majority of the world's population is female, women still find good reason to befriend males, and it goes beyond having different genitalia.

She can go to him for advice

When a woman is having relationship troubles and she wants a male perspective, it's eye-opening to speak to a man who can offer first-hand advice about her problem. A female friend can be there for her and listen to her weep, but chances are she doesn't have the masculine point of view that only a male friend can offer.

So when a guy she went on a few dates with doesn't call her after she finally sleeps with him, a male friend can tell her to move on if he doesn't call after night number five, while a female will go on a rant about how all men are jerks, or, worse, advise her to call him.

It's refreshing

While women can have a great time shopping all day, going for manicures together, and gossiping over a mocha cap, they also enjoy shooting pool with the boys, or even hanging out at a friend's bachelor pad to have a gangster movie marathon.

Take immediate action

If you're about to get serious with Jane, think about what you're getting into, so that when Jack, Joe, and Jeff come a-knockin', you're not sweating. Know that you're going to be sharing her with other guys from the start, or else you're bound to be unhappy later on.

Don't ever expect her to stop being friends with these men because you ask her to in the midst of your relationship—that could be grounds for a breakup.

If you want to nip it in the bud, ask her about her male friends early in your relationship: how they became friends, whether they're in her group of friends or not, or how long they've been friends.

Gather up your team

Take advantage of the fact that she has male friends by using them as your allies. You want to get her guy friends (and female ones, for that matter) on your good side, so that if and when you get into a fight, they don't assume you messed up because you're a jerk "and they always knew you were."

When you're out with her and her friends, act like you're interested in their lives, joke around with them, and always treat your girlfriend extra nice when they're all around. Be their friend, and they'll be yours when you need them most.

At the same time, you need to decipher which of her male friends have liked her in the past, and which have had an intimate encounter with her before you even came around.

If you show her that you're comfortable with all her buddies, and that any friend of hers is a friend of yours, she'll appreciate you and your security even more.

Identify the enemy

Some men who claim to "just be friends" with your girlfriend have ulterior motives. They're just waiting for the moment to slip the rug from under your feet and catch her in their arms, so you'll need to be alert to some warning signs that there may be trouble ahead:

He invites her to her favorite Broadway play

All she talks about is how much she'd give to go see *Hairspray,* and there her pal is, with two tickets to the play. You're thanking him for the tickets, when you find out the second ticket is for him, not you—you're just the understudy.

He cooks an elaborate meal for the two of them

She closed a huge deal at work and got promoted. You're excited to take her out for dinner to celebrate, but she's not hungry because her buddy just cooked veal, pasta, and fried zucchini . . . for a party of two.

He's always trying to one-up you

No matter what you do for her, you feel that he's always trying to upstage you. You buy your girlfriend a CD for your one-month anniversary; he buys her an iPod "just because."

He badmouths you

If you find out that he's badmouthing you from a reliable source, then you're dealing with someone who might just want the best for him, not for her. And if she begins quoting him in arguments, "Chris says you shouldn't be going out with your friends every Friday night," then tell Chris what you have to say about that.

He becomes her number one priority

If basketball games have always been a tradition for your girlfriend and her male friend, even before you came into the picture, you don't have much to worry about. But if she merely pencils you in whenever you make plans for the two of you, then her friend is probably becoming your enemy.

These are all my pals!

You knew her male friends consisted of Larry, Curly, and Moe, but all of a sudden she's talking about Brad, who she met at the photocopy store and just had coffee with.

As much as her candor is appreciated and you can't suspect her of cheating since she's being so honest with you, you can't help but raise an eyebrow when new men come into the picture.

You deserve to be suspicious because you know more than anyone else that men do not want female friends. They have their friends and aren't on the lookout for new females to add to their circle, unless, of course, they believe they stand a chance with her. In that case, a man will hang out with a woman under the premise of trying to befriend her, while actually trying to get her to fall for him.

Armed with this information, you need to find out how they became friends, and make sure they are indeed just pals. Ask her more about him (as in, "does he have his own girlfriend?"), and whether he knows about you (ask this in a joking manner).

Whether you like it or not, you can't stop her from making new friends, even if they are male. But if you're not happy about it, here's how you can handle it:

Ask her how she would feel

Tell her that although Brad sounds super-nice, you think it's a little strange that she's hanging out with a new male friend. If she doesn't understand what you're getting at, ask her how she would feel if all of a sudden you were having drinks with Pamela and helping Carmen move. If she claims it wouldn't bother her, she's either lying or she's a very odd bird. Don't jump at her and tell her that Brad just wants to get into her pants, just be honest and tell her you're not happy about it.

Ask her to be honest

You're being honest with her by telling her you're not pleased with the situation, and you should expect the same in return. Ask her to be honest, and remember, the more accusatory your tone is, the more reason it gives her to lie to you about her lunch dates.

Tell her you want to meet him

If you find that this guy just won't quit, tell your girlfriend to invite him out. You'll win bonus points because you seem open-minded and want to meet her new friend, and at the same time, it'll be your opportunity to show Brad that you and she are an item, and you're not stepping back.

Draw the line

If several new men come into her life and you're losing sleep at night, think about whether she's distancing herself from you. If her behavior has changed, ask her if everything's all right.

If her behavior continues and she doesn't take your feelings into consideration, tell her she'll have all the time in the world to be with her male friends, now that you'll be out of her life. You have to draw the line somewhere.

It's all about friendship

Your girlfriend's friends—male and female—will always be an issue for as long as the two of you date. It's always good to have all her friends on your side, and if you care about her, you'll want your friends to like her as well. Friends are a big part of both of you; they help to make up who you are.

Show her that you're comfortable with her close male friends and she'll appreciate you more. But when her male friends—new or old—become her number one priority, it's your duty to tell her how you feel about it. And if she refuses to budge, it's your turn to go find a new female "friend" of your own.

TOP 10 SIGNS YOUR BUDDIES HATE YOUR GIRL

Of course, *her* friends aren't always the problem. Guys are notorious for giving their buddies a hard time about spending time with their girlfriends. While usually this is just harmless teasing, sometimes it could be a sign that they sincerely don't like your girlfriend, a situation that could be detrimental to your friendship or your relationship.

Do your best pals secretly wish you would ditch your girlfriend?

Check out these telltale signs, and learn how to proceed if your suspicions turn out to be well-founded.

Number 10: They avoid you when you're with her

This seems like the most obvious sign, but sometimes we're too blinded by love to recognize when it's happening. When was the last time your friends accepted an invitation to hang out when you mentioned that she would be joining you? If it was a long time ago, it could mean that they're not too fond of her.

Number 9: They've stopped coming by since she moved in

Have your buddies kept their distance since she became your roommate? Even if she hasn't moved in, but spends most of her time at your place, you should take note of how that's affected the frequency of visits from your friends.

Number 8: They talk to you about other girls

While the ego boost might feel good, you should be suspicious about constant references to what a player you could be if you weren't attached. This might really just be a nice way of telling you that you could do much better than her.

Number 7: They always insist on a "guys' night out"

It's normal for friends to suggest a guys' night out once in a while. But if they insist that you leave the lady at home every time you hang out, it's probably a sign that they're not too crazy about her.

Number 6: They're uncomfortable alone with her

Has your girlfriend ever mentioned that your friends act awkward when they're left alone with her? Is she included in their conversations when you're not there? There is a point when you have to stop blaming it on her shyness. If your buddies and your girlfriend still feel uncomfortable around each other months into the relationship, take note.

Number 5: They tease you about being "whipped"

There's a fine line between a joke in passing and a pattern of consistent ridicule. If your friends are constantly teasing you about being controlled, it probably means that they genuinely believe it. And it also probably means that they resent her because of it.

Number 4: They argue with her in front of you

Do they fight about the smallest things? Can they ever agree on anything? It may seem like harmless bickering at first, but if your friends and girlfriend always seem to argue with each other, even about little things, it could be a sign of deep-seated tension.

Number 3: They constantly point out her bad behavior

Do your friends ever encourage you to be angrier than you think you should be about something she did? If they seem to think that she doesn't treat you well, chances are they don't support your relationship.

Number 2: They badmouth her friends

If your buddies are always talking about how much they hate her friends, it could just be their way of venting the negative feelings they really harbor for her. Maybe they'll point out how her girlfriends tease men for free drinks or can't stop talking about themselves. Whatever it is, your friends seem to have it in for hers.

Number 1: They sell you out

Do they talk a lot of trash about you to your girlfriend? This is a clear sign that they're trying, in essence, to get her to break up with you.

They hate her, now what?

If you're convinced that your friends really do hate your girlfriend, you have to take action before things get worse. Believe it or not, it's possible to salvage both relationships. Try using these tips:

■ Give your friends some of the attention they're craving. Call them more often and spend more of your time with them.

■ Keep 'em separated. If your friends and your girlfriend don't get along, don't try to force them to. Keep their mutual company to a minimum and enjoy the best of both worlds separately.

■ Accept the fact that your friends don't have to love her. After all, you're the one who's dating her.

She says: "I like your friends, but . . ."

She means: I don't like your friends.

Why she does this: She doesn't want to come off as controlling or insulting to you or your friends, so she's not going to tell you outright how much she dislikes them. She probably thinks they're a bad influence on you and wants you to hang out with them less.

What you should do: It depends on what she says she doesn't like about them. If she has a valid reason to dislike them, then you might take her concerns into consideration. Otherwise, simply tell her that your friends are important to you and that you'd like her to make more of an effort to get along with them.

In an ideal world, your best buddies and your soul mate would co-exist in perfect harmony. But we don't live in an ideal world, and the reality is that it's common for friends to dislike their buddy's girl.

What's important is that you don't sacrifice one relationship for the other—recognize the value in both relationships, and be willing to do what it takes to preserve them.

RULE 6
MAINTAIN YOUR RELATIONSHIP

When we're young and in our first relationships, it's easy to fall into the naïve belief that a romance can sustain itself; that love is unconquerable and that the magical power that gave rise to the initial attraction will suffice to fuel the pairing well into the future.

After a few failed relationships, however, this way of thinking quickly finds its way onto the dust heap. And as a man looks back on the part he played in these same failed relationships, it often emerges that it was less a question of what he did, and more a question of what he didn't do.

Guys, by nature, are lazy when it comes to relationships. So rather than relying on yourself to remember that it's time to offer up a gesture of your appreciation for her, read on and commit some of our maintenance tips to memory.

She says: "I feel like our relationship is stuck in a routine right now."

She means: I want you to be more romantic and spontaneous, and surprise me more. I need you to pay more attention to my needs.

Why she does this: She doesn't want to hurt your feelings and admit that you are, in part, the cause of the rut.

What you should do: You don't need to change your personality entirely, but it wouldn't kill you to surprise her every once in a while. Call her out of the blue and tell her you're taking her for dinner, go on a spontaneous weekend away, or just surprise her with her favorite chocolates.

PAINLESS RELATIONSHIP MAINTENANCE

All relationships require maintenance. Of course, different relationships require different types of maintenance, and some will require more time and attention than others. A relationship in trouble, for example, will need carefully tailored maintenance and consistent effort in order to repair it. However, if things are moving along generally smoothly in your relationship and you'd like to keep it that way, there are a few easy and efficient ways to grease the wheels with your lady without keeping you constantly occupied.

Before we begin, a special note: It's necessary to control the frequency and timing of these maintenance tips. After all, if you use them too often, you'll come off as insincere and flaky. Nonetheless, their use should be familiar and natural to you. Generally, a happy relationship should stay that way so long as you both feel respected and cared for. Here are a few quick and painless tips to keep your situation with the lady shipshape.

1. Compliment her with sincerity

Giving her a sincere compliment means that when she comes into the room and your heart skips a beat, you should let her know. Tell her that she's looking good and that she still does it for you in all the right ways (assuming that this is the case). Or, tell her that her recent promotion at work was well deserved, and that her boss is lucky to have her. These types of compliments are not over-the-top or excessively mushy, but they make her feel special and appreciated. Giving her such verbal assurances will help put her at ease and make her more relaxed around you, since she won't have to guess your sentiments. Knowing how you feel will boost her confidence, and because you're responsible for the improvement in her mood, you should be rightly thanked for it.

2. Fulfill one of her nagging requests

You know that thing that she consistently asks you to do—be it trimming that beard a little closer or taking her out for a nice dinner—and you always neglect to do it? Well, if you get up and do it, and do it consistently, she'll notice and she'll appreciate it. Doing such good deeds doesn't take much more effort than a little mindfulness, and they will keep her singing your praises. Not only will you be doing things that she likes, but you'll also be doing what she has asked, which is where the secret power of this maintenance tip is hiding. Doing things that she has requested will show her that you've actually been listening to her and not just to your sports recaps. Pick a few of her favorite wishes and try them out.

3. Surprise her

Just the little romantic gestures can make a very big difference to a relationship. If you know that she has had a long day, grab some coffee from the cafe she loves so much. If you're at the grocery store, pick up her favorite ice cream. The little gift doesn't need to be expensive or extravagant to please her; you just need to preemptively consider what she'll want, and try to give it to her. Pick things that are personalized to her tastes, emphasizing your intimate knowledge of her likes and dislikes. Behaving this way will make her especially happy when she receives your little tokens, and it will also show how special you think those little details are. For more information on the power of romantic gestures and tips for making them flawlessly, flip to The Life Span of Romantic Gestures on page 118 in this chapter.

4. Choose her over the boys

Let's face it: Many men get very touchy about giving up their night out with the boys. Your girl knows that this time is important to you, and most girls will give you the space to enjoy it. However, it is important that you recognize your girl as a priority in your life. This means that you'll have to occasionally promise her a movie night at home, and skip going out with the boys. A little goes a long way with this, so make sure she recognizes a visible sacrifice on her behalf. Because this might not always be obvious to her, it could be worthwhile to subtly bring it to her attention. Also, stay very clear of any hint of remorse on the decision; let her know that the boys were doing their thing, but you wanted to spend a little quality time with her.

5. Write her a note

The written word often packs a punch that a verbal message can't match. Little notes and messages give her visible proof and little keepsakes of your feelings, something she doesn't receive that often. These don't have to be sappy love notes to do the trick. Write a personal message inside a card on Valentine's Day instead of just signing it or leave a little note if you've dropped by her apartment. Even a little text message letting her know that she's on your mind can boost her day. Sign off with a little romantic gesture, such as with "yours" or "kisses" instead of "see ya later," showing her you don't think of her as one of the guys. Little written reminders that you're thinking of her will have a great deal of impact.

6. Hang out

Sometimes the big events, special as they are, are not where your relationship is solidified. Make the effort to simply share time together: Having movie night or bonding as you both yell at reality television will make the two of you feel as though you share more than popcorn at the movies. Spending some downtime together is a good way to keep a healthy handle on your identity as a couple, so that when you're among friends the bond remains tight.

She says: "You don't communicate enough."

What she means: How do you feel about me, and about our relationship?

Why she does this: She wants to know how you are feeling and where the relationship is going, but doesn't want to come off as needy. She is hoping you'll volunteer your thoughts and feelings on your relationship.

What you should do: Put her mind at ease and tell her what you think about the relationship. If you don't do it now, she'll just find another way to ask you.

Avoid a relationship overhaul

Generally, the key to relationship maintenance is to remind each other of your feelings. Performing small gestures along the way keeps you thinking of her, and keeps her in a forgiving mood—both of which will pave the road for a smoother relationship. Keep in mind that nothing that's been mentioned here is over the top, expensive, or life-altering. They're all small things that make up a big picture, and none of them will tax your mind or your pocketbook.

She says: "I want to do something together."

She means: We need more one-on-one time together.

Why she does this: She is saying it in this roundabout way to avoid coming off as needy.

What you should do: It depends how much time you are spending together. If you don't spend much time together, you can increase it. If you already spend most of your time together, you can ignore the hint. Remember: What you do early on in the relationship will set the tone for the rest of it, so don't feel that you have to give in to everything she demands

---

THE LIFE SPAN OF ROMANTIC GESTURES

While a romantic gesture is a big deal to any woman, you need to keep in mind that its effects aren't as long-lasting as you might think. Even the most spectacular gesture will wear off, and there is not a single romantic idea that will get you off the hook forever.

Because romance isn't always a natural endeavor for men, most will overestimate the lasting effects of a given gesture. The majority will consider the effort that they have put in to be good for a lifetime, but any guy will find himself in hot water if he tries to appeal to an angry girlfriend by reminding her of the flowers he bought for her—six months ago.

Bringing up your gesture history with your girlfriend will only serve to remind her exactly how long it's been since you did something thoughtful, so it's best to either keep up with the gestures on a regular basis or to extend the life of each and every romantic thought for as long as possible.

A sincere compliment

Life span: It'll last until you replace the compliment with a less flattering thought or comment, which for some klutzes could be the next time you open your mouth.

Make it last: Instead of pointing out fairly generic physical characteristics, try praising an accomplishment or a personality trait—meaning anything that is more specific to her—to come off sounding even more tuned in to her as an individual. For a truly great take on this, extend your praise to ears other than her own; talking her up to her friends or your buddies is sure to get back to her eventually, and she'll be even more flattered that you went out of your way to spread the word.

Impromptu flowers

Life span: This gesture will last as long as the buds themselves: a week or two at the most.

Make it last: Ignore the standard dozen red roses that seemed like a sure thing when you were eighteen, and create an individualized bouquet with her in mind. Your woman will appreciate flowers more if you handpick a bloom that has a little more to say. Has she mentioned any flowers before? What about a favorite color or vacation destination? Did you know that every birth month has a flower associated with it? Step into any florist to get an idea of the hundreds of combinations that are available and use your imagination. Not only will she get a bouquet with something a little more exotic and a little less clichéd than a standard arrangement, but explaining the significance of your choice will assure her that you put some thought into it.

Romantic dinner

Life span: You'll benefit from the effects of this gesture for about a month.

Make it last: Just about anyone can make a restaurant reservation, but not everyone can put in the time and effort to cook a meal from scratch—that means no frozen dinners or caterers allowed. Cooking for her will spark her desire to be with someone that can provide for her or at least share household tasks in the future without constant prodding and complaints. Keep in mind: The dinner doesn't have to be incredibly fancy or elaborate to make a point; the sheer sight of you in an apron puttering around the kitchen should do the job. For extra points, tell her you called your mom/aunt/grandmother for instructions on creating the dish. Don't forget to set a nice table and chill a bottle of white wine to highlight the special nature of the night.

Random gift

Life span: If it's truly unexpected, the impact of an out-of-the-blue gift can last for a few weeks or even a month.

Make it last: Guys who are truly tuned in know that presents on birthdays and holidays are just the starting point for men on a romantic mission; catching your lady off-guard with a gift will always leave her feeling swept away. Get the most out of the purchase by presenting her with something you know she wants or desires but wouldn't get for herself. Keep your eyes and ears open for items she admires but deems frivolous; if you surprise her with something that has no purpose other than to make her happy, you can score a more enduring impact. To really get the most out of any gift-giving situation, focus on items that are useful but extravagant and that will remind her of you and your thoughtfulness on a regular basis, like silk sheets or great-smelling body lotion.

Taking an interest

Life span: In general, this gesture is one of the few that is genuinely reciprocal in nature. For example, watching a television show she likes will get you one complaint-free viewing of a show of your choice.

Make it last: The golden rule is that you'll always come out a winner if you offer rather than give in: If she has to argue or convince you into sharing her hobbies or interests, the life span is pretty much down to nil. Go a step further with a little time-investment outside of the actual event in question to leave her with positive feelings that will last significantly past your initial attentive spurt. Does she like salsa dancing? Instead of just offering to take her out one night, try taking a few lessons without her knowing and then wow her with your dance-floor skills.

Looking after her in a time of illness/crisis

Life span: How you choose to deal with her when she's sick or going through a hard time can be a deal-maker or deal-breaker in most relationships. Opt to take care of her, and she'll never forget your thoughtfulness.

Make it last: Any guy that has been in a relationship will know that the duty of a loving boyfriend automatically means bringing tissues and soup to a girlfriend with the flu. This is one of the key areas that marks the difference between casual dating and genuine togetherness, and lets a woman know that even when sex isn't on the agenda, you're still around to help her out with the not-so-good parts of life. Flat tires, bathroom floods, or even a death in the family are times when boyfriends can really step up to the plate and cement some long-lasting romantic karma. To rev up the returns, extend your goodwill to include her loved ones, like a treasured pet or close family member. Something as simple as driving her mother to pick up a rental car after a traffic accident or scouring the city for a lost dog can put you in the boyfriend hall of fame for good.

Romantic moves

Romantic gestures are as old as romance itself, and there really isn't any excuse to simply rest on your laurels and put in the bare minimum of effort. Your woman expects you to be inspired enough to pull out a few tricks even after you've been together for a while. Don't worry, she isn't necessarily looking for sonnets or grand gestures of a cinematic caliber. To get the best return on your romantic investment, just remember to use a little originality and creativity to really make a lasting impression.

4 WAYS TO COMMUNICATE WITH WOMEN

A perfectly timed bouquet or a spontaneous weekend getaway will certainly inject freshness and vitality into your relationship. But the relative success of any romance depends not on the little surprises that you pepper it with, but rather on the kind of day-to-day exchanges you have in between them. Communication is the foundation and bedrock of your bond with other people. Communication: Can it get any more basic than that?

No. And as a result, you may assume that we are all experts in the field of good communication. Of course, such an assumption is false. Because, as we well know, the most common relationship predicaments arise from miscommunications.

All you have to do to prevent misunderstandings is communicate with your woman. A piece of cake, right? Well, most of us have learned from ugly experience that it's anything but. It's time to start remedying this chronic problem. Men, start with these tips:

1. Make time

That's right; make time. You set aside time to watch sports, eat, and have sex, don't you? Why should communication with your woman be any different? You have to block off an hour or two for quality time with her, whenever possible. Make the effort to sit down across from her after a long day to discuss work, friends, and your relationship. Heck, you can talk about the weather. Just talk.

Don't force the topic toward the relationship, but do seize the opportunity to mention how well things are going or perhaps bring up areas you need to improve on to give her what she needs. In addition, don't shy away from explaining to her what you need from her. Too many men have a problem with this.

Take the time as you sit together, cook together, travel together, or eat together to voice your dissatisfaction with certain aspects of the relationship. Just do it in a calm fashion, so as not to alarm her. Reassure her that you're happy (if that is the case) with the overall relationship; you just want one or two things to change. Whatever you want to discuss, just make the time for it, and make it a joint effort.

2. Be an active listener

You've read it before, but the truth is that many men still have absolutely no clue how to do it. It's not that hard to be an active listener, but it does require a few traits that men sometimes find elusive: patience, concentration, and modesty.

It requires patience because you have to give her as much time to elaborate on her message as she needs, point blank. Concentration is key, because not only do you have to look at her, but you also need to focus on her: her eyes, her body language, and her voice. What is she saying? What is she telling you? Concentrate.

Modesty is included because a lot of men have a problem letting someone take the floor for an extended period of time. They like to hear their own voice and want others to hear it, too. These men want to dominate the conversation and hold court, so to speak. This is not, sad to say, a trait conducive to good relationship rapport.

So toss your ego aside and let her speak. And above all else, let her have the last word once in a while. It's not a sign of masculine weakness to do so.

3. Let her know you care

This is where men get bitten in the behind. Our competitive nature compels us to try to win every fight, to the point where we forget the one simple tenet of relationship conflict: There is no winner. It's time to stop thinking of every fight as a chance to get the upper hand and flex rhetoric until she admits you're right.

That's not the end goal you should want in the long run. If it is, your woman will start to resent you before long. Not good. Let her know, no matter how bad, how intense, and how passionate the fight, that you care. Amidst all your rage and even when tempers flare, take a deep breath and do something to let her know that, when all is said and done, you love her.

Touch her arm, stroke her hair, put your palm to her cheek, or just say the words "I love you." Of course, some women don't appreciate such gestures in the "heat of battle" and may shove your hand aside or turn their back. Don't take it personally and don't get upset. Just get the message across that you care, even if she isn't ready to make up.

DO NOT BE ONE OF THESE GUYS

The Pretender

This is the man who has the appearance of an active listener, but at the end of the day does not give a damn about what his woman has to say. But give him credit; he manages to fool her almost every time. Too bad he has no idea how she feels at any given moment. His mind is on "more important" things, like fantasy football.

The Stage Hog

This big baby has to have all the attention, all the time. He loves to hear the sound of his own voice, to the detriment of his own relationship. Whenever possible, he shifts the focus of the conversation to himself, even if he has done his woman wrong. Do not become this loser.

The Trap-Setter

This selfish type listens to what he wants to hear. He is a selective active listener who turns the tables on his victim to use what she had to say against her at another point in time. His sole goal is to humiliate his woman the next time they fight and ensnare her to make himself look good. But who's watching? In the long run, nobody is.

The Contradictor

This type can take on many forms. He either refuses to acknowledge that there is a problem and unleashes a fierce temper until he gets his way, or worse yet, he turns his back anytime conflict arises. The bottom line, though, is that this guy can never take responsibility for his actions or recognize that something is amiss.

The Insensitive Jerk

This non-communicator can inhabit the body of any other type at any point in time. He is selfish and has his own agenda in mind every time he fights with his woman. For one reason or another, he refuses to show compassion or admit when he is wrong. He can be abusive in a verbal manner or, on the other side of the spectrum, hold his emotions in check so that his lady has no idea what is going on inside his small, dysfunctional head. Everyone hates Insensitive Jerk. Do not be him.

---

4. Remember that it takes time

Communication is a two-way street: It requires the proper delivery of a message, as well as an active listener to process it. If you keep that in mind and share with compassion and sensitivity, while holding that ego at bay, you should come out a winner.

9 COMMON RELATIONSHIP KILLERS

Once you've found the woman of your dreams, the last thing you want to do is lose her through a nasty misstep. Below are nine common relationship killers and how to avoid them.

1. Being critical

It is said that a little constructive criticism can be positive. This is the case, of course, for everybody except your girlfriend. Although suggestions are generally considered acceptable, particularly if she asks for them, putdowns and unwarranted negative input are expected from her mother, not her lover.

If you correct her, tell her how to dress, or generally act as though you know best, she will feel nitpicked and self-conscious. Every smart woman knows that she shouldn't spend her time with a man who doesn't make her feel good about herself. When in a relationship, be kind and generous, pick your battles, and give her advice only if she asks for it. Also, temper your criticisms with compliments.

2. Making it obvious that your career comes before her

Your job is important to you, and as such, it's important to your girlfriend. She's likely very proud of your successes and wants you to do well. On the other hand, if you start staying late at work every day, if you frequently cancel dates for last-minute business obligations, or if you constantly hang out with your co-workers after work hours, she will come to her own conclusions about your priorities.

Although a woman appreciates a focused and ambitious man, she also expects you to make time for her. Think of it this way: What fun is having a great career and lots of money if you have nobody to share them with?

3. Cheating

Physical cheating is never acceptable unless you and your girl have an agreement about such behavior. But cheating isn't limited only to sexual misconduct—there is a second type of cheating that can be nearly as hurtful. In this sense, read the word "cheating" as emotional cheating—committing to somebody else in a girlfriend-y way. This means having a female friend whom you relate to better than your girlfriend, that you spend more quality time with, or that you enjoy more.

This type of cheating applies to very serious relationships in which your girl would expect full disclosure and sharing. If you're relating that well to somebody else, chances are you're short-changing your girlfriend. This doesn't mean you can't have other friends or even other really close friends—it just means that your girlfriend wants to feel like you trust her and confide in her. She doesn't want to be second best. And if she is, she'll notice.

4. Becoming unkempt

Style is by no means infinitely important, but if you go from *GQ* to P.U. as soon as you're comfortable with her, she'll be sure to keep her distance. This tells her two things:

1. You were just putting on a façade to attract her

2. She's not important enough for you to maintain that façade

If she was attracted to you when you were wearing well-cut suits, chances are that's what she likes, and she may stop being attracted to you if all you wear are sweats and jerseys. If you're into sweats and jerseys, then that should be one of the first things she sees.

5. Being snappy

Now that you and your girl are getting closer, she's around more. And now that she's around more, her habits are becoming less novel and charming. You find yourself lashing out at her every so often and talking to her like she's your little sister. You act as though you're annoyed by her every move. You're not, of course, but you just feel comfortable enough to inform her of your preferences—bluntly.

Unfortunately for you, she probably won't accept this behavior for very long. Instead of being short with her, try to realize when you're getting annoyed. Then, decide rationally whether this particular annoyance is worth fighting over or not. If it's not, do your best to leave it alone. If it is, then calmly try to let your girl know. Chances are she'll be glad to know what bothers you, and she may even have a few suggestions for your habits.

6. Being controlling

It happens all the time. Many people in relationships suffer from fanatic "controlitis." You get jealous of her guy friends. You tell her not to spend so much time gossiping with her girl friends. You tell her she spent too much money at the shoe store. More than anything, you tell her where and when she should go out.

Although women have a reputation for being clingy, they also enjoy their independence. Chances are your girlfriend lived her life pretty successfully before you entered the picture. It is equally likely that she can still manage her own time and money without your help. There are situations in which she may want your input or advice, but otherwise, don't be pushy with advice or demands. Instead of demanding time, ask for it. Unless you want her to duck out when she sees you coming into a room, you have to give her space and let her make her own decisions.

7. Judging her friends and family

If you find her friends, her sister, and her mother annoying, you're going to have an awfully hard time. They're going to be around quite often, and she'll talk about them even more. It's important to try to see what she sees in them. If her posse is a bit shallow, try to find some substance, and if her mother is overbearing, try to realize she just wants to help. You have to understand that these people are her foundation and that she'll be very defensive about them. If you try to see the good things in them, you might actually start to like them.

Also, avoid direct confrontation with all her favorite people, even if they egg you on. Do your best to get along with those closest to her, because fights with them will translate into fights with your girl. If you can, become their favorite guy; it'll pay dividends in the end.

8. Becoming uninterested

Men often believe that the way to attract women is to be aloof. Even if that works in the beginning, it is certainly not the case once you become serious in a relationship. Your woman remembers what it's like to be wooed. She's also keenly aware of the fact that if you don't pay attention to her, a lot of other men will. If you stop complimenting her, taking her out, or asking about her life, she will feel neglected. Recognize that she doesn't have to be around you; you have to make it worth her while. If you want to keep her around, you need to make her feel like she's special. Look her in the eye. Call her in the middle of the day from time to time. When you think she looks pretty, tell her.

9. Not making time for her

You promised Joe you'd watch the game with him. You haven't been to the gym enough lately. You have to run errands. Although you may want to do all of the things you did when you were a bachelor, you also have to make time for your girl. It's tough, but sometimes you and your girl will both have to give up time with pals in order to spend time together.

It's all about the small things

If you want to keep a woman around, you should make her feel important, special, and competent. Any of the behaviors listed above will indicate that you're taking her for granted—and if there's anything a woman hates, it's being taken for granted. So make those small gestures; after all, if she's worth keeping, it shouldn't even feel like an effort to you.

RELATIONSHIP CHANGES WOMEN HATE

As you become more comfortable with her, feel free to be at ease, but be mindful not to commit any of the following relationship sins.

1. You start "letting go" around her

Why she hates it: Most couples attain a level of comfort in a long-term relationship where they don't hesitate to unleash the occasional fart or burp around each other. Although she probably doesn't mind this type of intimacy occasionally, if you consistently subject her to your bodily functions, she will start to dislike it, and her attraction may start to wane. She will feel like you see her as one of your boys instead of someone who is special to you.

2. You start forgetting big dates like birthdays and anniversaries

Why she hates it: You used to make a big deal for her birthday, and now you barely remember to call her. From her perspective, this lack of consideration shows her that you are progressively putting less effort into the relationship and taking her for granted. Remember that taking her out to celebrate is a big way to keep the romance going.

3. You stop complimenting her

Why she hates it: Do you notice when she changes her hairstyle or when she gets a new dress? Well, tell her. If you stop giving her compliments, she'll feel that you've stopped noticing her altogether. A woman needs a certain amount of attention and positive feedback from her man. If she's not getting it from you, she may start to look elsewhere for that attention, so don't forget to remind her how hot she is.

4. You don't compromise

Why she hates it: You used to be happy to spend time with her family, but now you're not as willing. Or maybe you used to put up with seeing the occasional romantic comedy and now you only want to watch action flicks. If you used to make compromises, but now you're completely inflexible, you might want to reconsider your change of behavior.

RULE 7
HANDLE THE TOUGH TIMES

In spite of your best efforts to foster a happy, healthy relationship with your woman, you will inevitably hit some rough patches together. Jealousy, arguments, breakups, and reconciliation—some of it will be her fault, some of it will be yours, and some issues will develop so abruptly that you won't even know where they came from.

These bust-ups aren't pleasant, but they are inescapable—and oftentimes, they can be beneficial to the relationship in the long term. Conflicts point to ongoing issues and provide the opportunity to resolve them permanently. So don't dodge the debate or try to sweep it under the carpet; instead, look at it as a chance to strengthen your romance. Let's look at some common relationship conflicts and ways to manage them.

OVERCOMING JEALOUSY IN RELATIONSHIPS

There is no quicker poison to a happy relationship than jealousy. Simultaneously suggestive of distrust, insecurity, and emotional fragility, jealousy can be an extremely destructive emotional force, and it's usually us guys who are guilty of introducing it. Whether it's because of our competitive natures or just because we know how sly we can be, we men are too quick to see betrayal where there isn't any, and the unfortunate product of this tendency is a self-fulfilling prophecy: Oftentimes, our irrational fear of seeing our woman with another man is what ultimately propels her there.

Many a man before you has lost his otherwise great relationship to his own base impulses. Get yours in check and avoid joining them.

Jealousy scenario: The two of you are seated in a restaurant. She is looking like her usual sexy self, and you marvel at the fact that you're with the hottest woman in the room. Everything is going great until a male model wannabe makes his way through the crowd and stops at your table. Your lady looks up and is elated to see her former flame. As she introduces you, you try to maintain a smile while shaking hands.

They continue to exchange friendly words and you sit idly by while your blood boils to levels that may or may not result in his body being flung over to the dessert cart. In short, his mere presence is making you lose it.

Sound familiar?

This scenario is one of millions that depict jealousy, an emotion we all instinctively experience at some point or another. Just like aggression and paranoia, jealousy can take on varying degrees of severity. The aforementioned scene could result in your either calming yourself into being at ease with the ex's presence, or getting into an all-out brawl with the guy, while accusing your date of being a tramp for having responded to his greeting.

For some, jealousy is a real issue, and if left untreated, it can create a permanent wedge between you and your partner, and negatively affect future relationships. Luckily, it can also be controlled.

What is jealousy?

Taken literally, jealousy refers to a strong desire for someone else's stature or possessions. But in a social setting, it causes someone to be doubtful of their partner and feel threatened by their interaction with certain people, the clothes they wear, or the places they go.

There are varying degrees of jealousy:

Cute jealousy

Jealousy does not necessarily merit negative connotation. After all, it's normal for men to be somewhat possessive of their women (and vice versa). Having reservations about her going to a strip bar with friends or not enjoying the sight of her drooling over some guy in a magazine are innocent examples of how some jealousy can be harmless, and a normal reaction.

Healthy jealousy

Likewise, a man who voices his concern over letting his girlfriend go out with a bunch of guys or seeing another man flirting with her is also part of a healthy relationship. Oftentimes, a man is just looking out for his girlfriend's well-being, and women usually respect that. They may even be insulted if you don't say anything.

Obsessive jealousy

The problem arises when aggression and/or violence accompanies the jealousy. Once you've reached this stage, you obsessively begin questioning her loyalty to you and reacting angrily to the scenarios that you conjure up in your own mind.

You develop an extremely low tolerance level and, before long, she is unable to even look at another guy or leave your side when you're both out. You demand to know where she is at all times, and the mere mention of another guy's name sends you off the deep end.

She says: "A man was flirting with me all night."

She means: Does it make you jealous?

Why she does this: She wants you to know that she's a hot commodity and that other men are interested in her. She wants you to appreciate what you have.

What you should do: Don't respond to it in a way she'll expect, like by getting angry or jealous. Instead, pay her a compliment—she's definitely fishing for it. Don't get all insane with jealousy; just let her know what she means to you, or else she'll be playing this card every so often to set you straight.

The source of jealousy

You may have acquired your jealous behavior through past experiences with girlfriends. If you have already been cheated on, this may cause you to be more possessive and controlling of her for fear of repetition. Even if she's never given you any reason to doubt her, you become increasingly desperate to hold on to the relationship and want to avoid potentially hazardous situations at all costs.

Similarly, you may be the one who's been unfaithful in the past, and, in a desire to not have the tables turn on you, you want to ensure that you are the sole object of her interests.

But for the most part, jealousy is a by-product of one's own issues with self-confidence and self-esteem. You may feel that you're not good enough for her and that you're together by some freak accident. Most other guys may seem better looking to you and you feel threatened by that.

Watching her interact with other men leaves you feeling worried that she may be "stolen" from you. If you've only been with her a short time, you may even be bothered by the close bond she has with her male friends, whom she's known all her life.

Why is jealousy dangerous?

Jealousy, for those unable to control it, is detrimental to a relationship because it eats away at the one thing that holds it together: trust. To tell your girlfriend or wife that she cannot have lunch with a male co-worker is to tell her that you don't trust her (unless she has really given you reason not to). If you have to impose so many restrictions, should you two even be together?

Jealousy also takes away from your quality time together as it undoubtedly leads to numerous fights wherein you only focus on each other's negative qualities, even if they're only imaginary ones.

Furthermore, you end up wasting your time foolishly thinking up scenarios in which she may cheat on you. Before you know it, the greater part of your relationship will be spent on what could be happening rather than what is happening.

Jealousy will be harder to control as the relationship progresses, so if yours is reaching dangerously high levels, take steps to resolve it as soon as possible.

She says: "I really like that guy's hair."

She means: I don't like yours.

Why she does this: She figures that it's a lot nicer to hint at this than to tell you outright.

What you should do: Get a second opinion on your hair. She may be right that it needs a change. But if your second opinion tells you otherwise, feel free to stick to your guns and your hairstyle. In that case, just pretend that you didn't get her hint.

Learn to control yourself

Here are some ways to get a grip on your jealousy before you lose control and do something you may later regret:

1. Learn from past experiences

Look at how your behavior affected past relationships and use those hard lessons to help you behave better. You may soon discover that these tantrums are the cause of your troubled love life. Realize that getting upset with her without reason won't help your situation.

2. Deal with reality

Focus on what is really happening, not on what you perceive to be happening. With time, you may end up having difficulty distinguishing fact from fiction, and you don't want to kill an otherwise perfect relationship over things that never really happened. Don't let your imagination overrule the kind of person she really is.

3. Respect yourself

Realize that she chose you for a reason and there is no need for her to be so easily tempted elsewhere. Remind yourself that you're every bit as deserving as those guys you feel threatened by.

4. Get a third party's opinion

Ask a friend to take note of your behavior around your girlfriend. It may help you to fully understand the extent of your actions (as well as hers) by getting a neutral party's perspective.

5. Set some rules early on

Try establishing some general guidelines as to what is and what isn't acceptable for you. You don't need to share these with your lady—in fact, it's probably better if you preserve them as internal mental notes. These will act as stable, consistent protocols for you to reference when your mind gets whipped into a jealous frenzy.

6. Don't overreact

It's okay to feel jealous, as long as you can contain and channel it in a positive manner. Keep in mind that having other guys flirt with your girlfriend is normal; just consider it flattery. As long as he looks but doesn't touch, what's the big deal?

Remember that trust is the foundation of any relationship, and you shouldn't let your insecurities destroy yours. More important, show the lady the same respect you would want her to show you. If you can do as you please, then so can she.

THE ROOTS OF JEALOUSY

In order to conquer a problem, you need to understand it. Here are some of the common circumstances that give rise to jealousy in men.

- **Past experience:** Your last girl cheated on you, and you've been on high guard ever since.

- **Projection:** You're a player yourself, so you assume that she's going behind your back as well.

- **You're not used to a social woman:** The woman who's always around friends, both male and female, is a foreign concept, and is therefore untrustworthy.

- **You're insecure:** Let's face it: You don't think you're good enough for her, so you go crazy with the thought of losing her.

- **You're a pessimist:** You think that all good things must come to an end, and this one surely will. That is, unless you make an ass of yourself trying to prolong it with excessive protection.

■ **She told you about her past:** So she's an experienced one and her old flames are still in town. The thought of her sleeping with ex-boyfriends drives you nuts.

■ **She always wants to have sex with you:** Here's one you didn't expect: Her uncanny sexual appetite gets you green-eyed. You fear that if you're not around, she'll want to have sex with another guy.

DEALING WITH A JEALOUS GIRLFRIEND

While we guys are typically the jealous ones in relationships, that doesn't mean that women are immune to it. Jealousy is a two-way street. Her irrational feelings of envy can be just as destructive as yours, and there's a good chance that she'll be more vocal about them.

Before determining how to manage your girlfriend's jealousy, let's look at some examples of how this ugly emotion can manifest itself in women.

Exhibit A

On a clear Sunday afternoon, Jeff decides to go for a walk with his girlfriend, Clara. Lo and behold, there is a beautiful red Ferrari parked on the street.

Jeff can't help but stare at this wonderful work of art. He stops walking and turns his head a full 90 degrees to fully appreciate the magnificent machine.

When he finally snaps out of his trance, he raises his head. To his horror, there is a beautiful brunette wearing a tight white T-shirt and a really short skirt walking on the opposite side of the street.

Jeff swallows his saliva. He knows that he is in big trouble with his girlfriend.

In less than two seconds, Clara loses her mind and screams, "Bastard! How can you disrespect me by looking at another woman while I'm around you? I'll bet you want to screw her. So you wanna be with her? Then run to her like the dog you are!"

Exhibit B

During a corporate Christmas dinner, an unsuspecting gentleman by the name of Tom Jones introduces his wife Linda to his beautiful co-worker, Anita.

> TOM: Honey, I'd like you to meet Anita. She's probably the company's greatest asset.
>
> LINDA: (Thinking to herself, "Judging by the size of her breasts, I can see why she's such a great asset.") Hello Anita, it's such a pleasure to finally meet you.
>
> ANITA: Oh, hi, Mrs. Jones, it's really nice to finally meet you, too. Your husband has told me so many nice things about you.
>
> LINDA: (Thinking to herself, "I knew the dog was spending too much time with her. I wonder what else he's said about me.") Really? Well, thank you for sharing that with me.
>
> TOM: Wow, I knew the two of you would get along well. Sweetie, maybe you can invite Anita over for dinner sometime and cook that special lasagna of yours. You know, the one I love so much.
>
> LINDA: (Thinking to herself, "I can't believe he wants to bring this blonde bimbo into my home.") That's a great idea. Anita, you definitely must come over for dinner sometime.

During the car ride home, Linda can no longer contain her anger and explodes at her husband.

LINDA: So how long has this been going on between the
two of you?

TOM: What in God's name are you talking about?

LINDA: Oh, come on, I saw the way you looked at her. Don't
tell me you haven't banged her at the office.

TOM: Where do you come up with this nonsense?

LINDA: I'll bet she sleeps with all the men at the office.

Signs of jealousy

The plights of Jeff and Tom serve as examples of extreme jealousy. And
while not all envious outbursts are of this magnitude, jealousy has a tendency to amplify itself over time, meaning that today's snarky remark
may lead to tomorrow's public outburst. Nip all this nastiness in the bud
by learning how to recognize some of the early, more innocent signs of
jealousy.

■ She calls you every two hours just to say, "I love you," but it
seems like a premise to check up on you.

■ She has difficulty accepting that you have female friends.

■ When you get home from your boys' night out, she wants to
know all the details.

■ She gets visibly uncomfortable every time you come within
fifty feet of another attractive woman.

■ She questions you about your female co-workers.

■ She tries to trap you with questions like, "Do you find her
pretty?"

If you've experienced three or more of these signs, it's time to take
action. However, don't end a perfectly good relationship because your

girlfriend is a little jealous. Sure, too much jealousy can destroy a partnership, but a little jealousy can enrich relationships, spark passion and romance, and strengthen a couple's devotion to one other. Therefore, you shouldn't panic if your partner shows some signs of jealousy. As long as you don't feel scared, stressed, or like you're walking on eggshells, you don't have to worry.

If you do feel that her jealousy needs to be curbed, a good first step would be to look at which of your own actions may be aggravating this emotion in her. That's not to say that you should blame yourself for her irrational delusions. But let's be honest with ourselves: We guys tend to have wandering eyes, and if your girl is prone to jealousy to begin with, your male instincts are only going to make life more difficult for yourself. So try to steer clear of the following situations.

Looking at other women

When walking with your woman, noticing beauty is natural—just have the decency to be subtle about it and don't ogle.

Solution: If it's a sunny day, wear sunglasses so that your wandering eyes can gawk all they want. Just don't turn your head.

Having female best friends

Your girlfriend will most likely be jealous if your best friend happens to be another woman. She won't be able to help but wonder what you've done with her in the past and what may happen in the future. But this is no reason to end a great friendship.

Solution: Keep your friendship with the other woman, but prioritize your love life; don't be touchy with your best friend and always pay more attention to your girlfriend. Most important don't continuously talk about your best friend with your lover.

Paying too much attention to your friend's girlfriend

At times, your buddy might have a better-looking woman. There is no question your girlfriend will be well aware of this. So don't spend your double date drooling over your friend's girl.

Solution: Pay attention to your woman and never act in what could be perceived as a flirtatious manner with one of her female rivals.

Offering poor excuses

Most men use the same line over and over again when they go out with the boys: "I had a horrible time. The night was just not the same without you." Yes, that's right, and my dog is a vegetarian. Women are not stupid.

Solution: Be honest—but not too honest. Tell her that you had a good time with your buddies, but that nothing compares to hanging out with your favorite girl.

Comparing her to other women

A man will often shoot himself in the foot by trying to compliment his woman in comparison to other women. Avoid saying things like, "Of all the women here, you have the sexiest legs." She'll think that you're constantly comparing her to other women and will wonder how the rest of her body parts compare to theirs.

Solution: Compliment her without comparing her. Simply say, "You have sexy legs."

Being infatuated with female celebrities

Yes, if you had the chance to sleep with Angelina Jolie, you probably would. But your woman doesn't have to know this. Stop talking about your favorite celebrity and how many times you dream about her.

Solution: Simple: Your fantasies about celebrities should remain in your head.

Being too interested in adult material

Your watching porn or looking at pictures of naked women in magazines can make your woman feel unappreciated and insecure.

Solution: If she's not comfortable with it, don't do it in front of her.

Suggesting physical changes

Some men tell their girlfriends that they should change their hair from black to blond, wear colored contact lenses, or get breast implants. How would you feel if your woman told you to get a penis enlargement?

Solution: Accept your girlfriend as she is.

Healthy vs. extreme jealousy

As long as you appreciate your girlfriend and treat her with the respect that she deserves, there should be no reason for her to doubt your intentions. Sure, a little jealousy can help the relationship, but if you're acting like the perfect gentleman and she still doubts your actions, it may be time to reevaluate your relationship.

5 TIPS FOR ARGUING WITH WOMEN

Jealousy is but one of many potential points of contention within a relationship. Money, lifestyle habits, friends . . . the list is an endless one, and there's little value in trying to prepare a tailored remedy for each possible scenario. You can, however, train yourself in the discipline of clashing in a productive manner.

Fights are a risky business and, if not handled appropriately, can plant the seed for the relationship's demise, creating an atmosphere of resentment and hostility. These wars of words must be handled responsibly and with tact. To weather the storms and stay the course in a relationship, try the following rules of engagement.

1. Do not go in for the kill

This may be a war of sorts, but it should remain civil at all times. Whether it's a tête-à-tête at Camp David or a spat with the girlfriend at a summit of your own in the bedroom, any outcome that is too one-sided can end in failure or breakup.

When it's painfully obvious how justified you are in getting upset after she grilled you about chatting with the waitress that evening, for example, resist the temptation to rub the sweet victory in her face and allow her to leave the fight with dignity.

Should you go for the jugular with a demoralizing blow to the ego, you may come away feeling pretty clever and tough, but your triumph won't lend itself to reconciliation.

2. Stay relevant

Arguments between couples are invariably filled with emotional outbursts—yes, even for alpha males. That's why it's highly recommended that you stick to the topic you're arguing about. Do not bring up unrelated issues or suddenly interject, "Well, maybe you should go find that loser who dumped you three years ago because you were fat."

And should your woman try to stray from the topic, take charge of the situation and bring her back to the topic at hand. Remember, women have extraordinary memories, and if you're not careful, yours may attempt some Jedi mind-trick on you to put you on the defensive. Insist on dealing with one matter at a time.

3. Concentrate on the end result

Men are supposed to be the rational ones, so keep this in mind when it comes time to spar verbally. Decide what you are arguing about and what you hope to achieve by the end of it. If you don't have a clear understanding of your goals, how will you know when you've accomplished them?

Once your objectives are logically determined, ensure that when they are realized, the dispute ends. Nobody enjoys arguments that go in circles and never seem to end. Don't be part of the problem. When you've accomplished what you set out to do, make your woman aware that the train stops here and that you're not in the mood for a round-trip back to Nag Land.

4. Don't get personal

If your goal is to be constructive, allowing the argument to degenerate into name-calling and one-upmanship will not win you a Nobel Peace Prize. Even women who are rough around the edges usually take vulgarity directed at them to heart, whether they demonstrate it openly or not. You wear the pants, so be a man and keep your cool.

5. Pick your battles

There is always a decision to be made between two things that men value: being right, and peace and quiet. Every additional argument you commit yourself to decreases your football game–watching time by twenty minutes to an hour, depending on your woman. During the play-offs, the stakes are higher, naturally.

At the same time, though, it's difficult to just put down the gloves and take one on the chin. Our competitive nature provides a strong incentive to jump into the fray.

Choose where you want to direct your energies wisely, and be sure to adjust your intensity according to the importance of the topic. When it's not worth it, keep it low-key, or just let it go and who knows, you might be lucky enough to fall off the mood swing radar altogether.

She says: "I'm not angry."
She means: I'm angry.
Why she does this: If she's pursing her lips and not speaking to you, but claims she's not angry, she's probably bluffing. She could simply be bottling up her anger or she may think that her man should just know why she's upset, without her having to tell him.

What you should do: Try to figure out why she's upset and talk about it. The issue is not going to go away. In fact, if you don't deal with it now she'll just have pent-up anger toward you and it'll come back to bite you later.

FIGHT CIVILLY

Let's continue our fight training by looking at some specific techniques that can be applied in order to resolve disputes quickly and minimize the damage.

Get to the bottom of it

It's important to find out what's really wrong instead of dancing around the issue. Chances are that if something isn't dealt with, it will come up again. The sooner you focus on one issue and resolve it, the nicer the fight will be, and the sooner it will be over.

Focusing isn't always the easiest task, because in order to recognize the starting point of an argument, it is necessary to ignore the sideways insults that are thrown at you and to contain your own anger. This may be the hardest part of patching up a fight (aside from apologizing) because when insults start flying, it can sometimes feel as though there's no turning back.

The easiest way to get around this is to concentrate on getting your relationship back to normal. Remember that the person you're fighting with is someone you care about and would like to spend more time with. This will humble you and help you focus on the issue at hand. After all, a fight seems like a huge deal at the time, but in the grand scheme of things, it's only a hiccup.

Don't blame unnecessarily

No matter what your conflict is about, it is easy to justify your part in it so that you feel entirely innocent. This is dangerous because a high-and-mighty mindset can cause you to be more insulting than you should be. Just remember that, regardless of how a fight started, it takes more than one person to keep it going. This means that you're not entirely innocent. Some things are nobody's fault, and some things are your fault. Either way, assigning or accepting blame usually won't get you any closer to a resolution. In fact, it generally only makes people more defensive and angry. Instead, talk about what's wrong and what can be done to fix it.

Use "I" phrases

Instead of assuming that you know what's going on in somebody else's head, just say honestly what's happening in yours. For instance, saying, "I feel stressed out because I have to work really hard to pay the bills," will help to patch things up a lot more than, "If you didn't have such expensive tastes, I wouldn't have to work so damn hard." The latter will obviously put her on the defensive and bring on more nastiness, whereas the former says the same thing, but in a less confrontational way.

Using statements that begin with "I" also shows that you're willing to accept some responsibility, and you'll be less likely to exaggerate. This tactic is tried-and-true, as long as the "I" statement is not used to disguise an accusation, as in, "I feel like your expensive tastes are sucking me dry." If you use this technique wisely, you can speak from your own perspective to get good results rather than accusations and finger-pointing.

State your case

Make sure to clearly state your side of the argument. This doesn't mean you should be a jerk. You should be straight about what made you angry instead of just insulting her or pouting. You want to make sure that whatever caused the fight is addressed, so you need to be clear about what needs to change.

Since fights are so uncomfortable, many people tend to shy away from them or fly off the handle and yell about anything that makes them angry. Nothing constructive will come out of either approach. Think of a fight as an opportunity to make things better between the two of you; after all, it's not every day that you get to hear what she really thinks. Try to listen to what's bothering her and tell her everything that's on your mind. Some things might be hard to say, but think of it this way: If you get the problem out in the open, you will probably be able to solve it.

Swallow your pride

Fights can sometimes go on and on because neither person will back down. Nobody wants a fight to continue, but in the heat of the moment, many people don't realize that just making a nice, understanding comment or gesture can sometimes be the answer. This doesn't mean giving in to the other's point of view; it simply means that one person needs to be the one to take the fight down a notch. This can require apologizing for your part in the argument, but it can also simply be a question of facing the problem more calmly. Chances are that if you chill out, the whole fight will take on a new tone and it will be easier to fix things up.

See her side

Listen to what she has to say because, as they say, there are two sides to every story. You don't need to bow down in order to hear what she has to say; just make sure that while you're making your point, you're also hearing hers. If you don't, she might give in because she sees she's not getting anywhere, but she'll still be angry and the issue won't be resolved. Don't let your anger cloud your hearing, and when she says something, respond to it. This will minimize the length of the fight because you'll both be getting points across in record time.

Fight like a civil man

In a nutshell, listen and talk fairly in an argument—it will keep things civil and get the problem dealt with quickly. When you're in a fight, it can be hard to play nice, but sometimes a small gesture goes a long way. Buying flowers for your angry girlfriend won't get you out of trouble, but they're likely to soften her anger. After all, if you're interested in retaining a relationship after the fight, a thoughtful gesture lets her know that you're really interested in making it better.

TOP 10 ARGUMENTS TO AVOID

No matter how successful you become at managing them, arguments in general are something that you'll naturally want to steer clear of. And arguments concerning these ten hot-button female issues are ones that you'll definitely want to avoid.

Stay away from these ten biggies and you'll save a lot of time and energy.

Number 10: Her style

Not only does your girlfriend feel it's her right to make sure you're dressed appropriately, but she also sees it as her responsibility to make sure you look good. However, just because she does it to you, it doesn't mean she wants you to do it to her. In fact, you should avoid all and any negative clothing references. Comments like, "Isn't that a little too short/low-cut/small?" should be deleted from your vocabulary. Yes, it's a double standard, but who said that relationships were fair?

She says: "How do I look in this [insert clothing item]?"

What she means: I need more reassurance from you.

Why she does this: She is somewhat insecure and needs more reassurance than you've been giving her. She really wants to hear a "you look beautiful/hot/wonderful" from you.

What you should do: Tell her what she wants to hear, unless she is modeling a particularly ill-fitting item of clothing. (You want to bend the truth here, not tell a flat-out lie.)

Number 9: Her cooking

Not every woman can make spaghetti sauce like your mom, but under no circumstances should you compare their recipes. That's rule number one. The second commandment is: Never insult her cooking. Even if it's charred to high heaven, just chew and smile and remember that it's the thought that counts.

Number 8: Her exes/your exes

No good can come of bashing her ex-boyfriend. He may not be the best guy, he may even have cheated on her, but speaking ill of her past will only make her defensive. It's her life; it's her mistake, so leave it at that. In turn, don't even think about comparing your past and present girlfriends. You're treading on very dangerous territory.

Number 7: Gender generalizations

Do you and your girlfriend get in a fight every time you get in the car? If so, it may be because you insult her driving or navigational skills. She may not study the map like you, but when you accuse her of driving like a woman, this will make her want to fight with you. Other gender generalizations to avoid include women being too emotional or too verbal.

Number 6: Her finances

Your money is not her money, and hers is not yours. So if she wants to spend $250 on a pair of designer jeans, that's her prerogative. You may not approve of her purchases, but unless her spending habits are personally and negatively affecting you, you're better off keeping mum about it.

Number 5: Her friends

If you don't have anything nice to say about her friends, don't say anything at all. Yes, they might be gossipy, or even petty, but pointing this out will only drive a wedge between the two of you.

Number 4: Your solutions to her problems

When she complains about her misogynist boss, you—being the nice guy that you are—offer up a couple of ways to remedy the problem. Your intentions are good, but she gets mad. Why? She isn't telling you her problem you so you'll fix it for her, she just wants to vent—and when you jump in with advice (common guy blunder), she gets insulted. Instead, just listen and nod. Remember: She wants your support, not your advice.

She says: "Why do you wash the dishes/clean the floor/fold clothes like that?"

She means: You are doing it wrong.

Why she does this: She doesn't want to discourage you by telling you that you're doing household chores wrong or not in the way that she likes. She wants you to keep helping out with chores, but do it her way.

What you should do: Do it her way; it'll be less of a hassle in the long run.

Number 3: Her appearance

If you haven't figured it out already, women are sensitive about their appearances—especially their weight and hair. So if she's having a fat day and asks you the typical loaded question, "Does my butt look big in these pants?" she doesn't really want you to be honest, she just wants reassurance that you love her no matter what.

She says: "Your love handles are so cute."

She means: Get rid of them, please.

Why she does this: Most women know what it's like to struggle with body issues, so she would never insult you by telling you that you need to head to the gym. This way, she's letting you know that you do indeed have love handles, but in a kind and gentle way. (Note: There may be a small percentage of women who are sincere when they compliment your love handles. How do you tell the difference? It's all in her tone.)

What you should do: This one's up to you. Don't go to the gym simply to please someone else (love handles generally are not deal-breakers, anyway). But feel free to go if it will please you.

Number 2: Her family

There's a pretty simple rule when it comes to her family: Put up and shut up. Even if you're just agreeing with something she says or joking around, she's likely to take anything negative you say about them personally because when you insult a girl's family, you insult the girl.

Number 1: Her PMS

The fastest way to start an argument is to ask the dreaded question, "Are you having your period?" Yes, she may be acting a tad emotional (okay, she's downright erratic), but pointing out her hormone-fueled behavior will only send her over the edge. This is because, although she may be overreacting, if you bring up her PMS, you're dismissing whatever she's saying as just "wacko crazy time-of-the-month talk."

You're never going to understand it (neither does she), so there's no sense in going to war over it. It's a no-win situation.

THE ABCs OF RELATIONSHIP RECOVERY

You did it again. You started an argument about one of the ten aforementioned taboo topics, you forgot her birthday or your anniversary, you got caught flirting with another girl, you stood her up because of car trouble, or you stood her up because you forgot. Whatever the crime, now you have to do the time.

How can you bounce back from your relationship no-no and regain her trust and affection?

If you're on the outs after a particularly spectacular argument, the formula for winning her over all over again is as simple as the alphabet. Follow these ABC of relationship recovery and you'll be able to rebound from almost any misstep.

A. Admit you made a mistake

Once it's clear that you've been caught, and there's absolutely no way to wiggle out of the consequences of your misdeed, you might as well admit to it. Come clean about the screwup and try to deal with the situation as it is. If you lie about the details at this stage, odds are she'll either sense that you're not being entirely honest with her, or she'll hear another version of the story from someone else.

For example, if she hears through the grapevine that, after a couple of drinks, you were a little too cozy with a female co-worker at an office party, and you know that there's some truth to this story, don't outright deny it. Face the music. Admit that it might have looked that way to outsiders, but blame the booze and say you were "just letting off some steam and have no interest in that girl whatsoever," or something similar.

Be straightforward, but don't be stupid. Downplay your mistake as much as possible. Remember, she wants very badly to believe that you didn't let her down, so use those hopes to your advantage. Even if an excuse sounds lame to you, she might still buy it if you present your points convincingly.

In these situations, there can be such a thing as too much honesty. For example, while you definitely should admit that you went a little too far at the office party, you don't have to volunteer the fact that you've always found that blonde in the sales department really attractive. Damage control means minimizing the mistake, not magnifying it by giving her more information than she needs to know.

B. Be sincere

When trying to recover a relationship, you can ruin everything by apologizing in an indifferent, sloppy way. Be genuine. Show through your tone and expression that you are genuinely sorry for your mistake, and that it will never happen again in the future. Make it clear to her that you are repentant of your crimes (even if you secretly think that they weren't that major).

The truth is that a woman is extremely susceptible to a man who seems heartbroken and remorseful. So if you forgot her birthday, and she's the type to be crushed by such an error, don't compound your mistake by shrugging it off and offering an "oops, sorry, no big deal" response. Instead, act serious and a little disappointed in yourself. If you adopt a casual or a defiant attitude at this stage, you risk prolonging the problem.

C. Compensate

Although it may seem a little transparent to compensate for bad behavior with special gifts or favors, if done with discretion and style, this is an excellent way to make amends. The key, as always, is presentation. Make up for being inconsiderate by showing just how thoughtful you really are. Give her the little pendant she eyes every time you walk by that boutique, or spend a night doing something she's always trying to get you to do but that isn't really your thing. One night of musical theater never hurt anyone and is really only a small sacrifice overall in the maintenance of a good relationship.

Keep in mind that you don't have to break the bank to win her back. Women are suckers for gifts that show that you've put time and effort into pleasing her. A copy of her all-time favorite childhood book is a romantic and sweet gift; a new DVD player, on the other hand, although useful, is not, and also gives the impression that you're just throwing money at a problem to make it go away. Choose your compensation gifts wisely.

D. Don't be a repeat offender

Even after you've accomplished A, B, and C successfully, you can ruin everything by making the exact same mistake again. Being rude to her friends once might just mean that you had a bad day and were short-tempered, but acting like a jerk on a regular basis proves that . . . well, you're a jerk. Prove that you've "learned your lesson" by making an extra effort to avoid it in the future.

For example, if you know that you have a tendency to get distracted by whatever you're doing and are often late for dates, set an alarm, and give yourself a lot of time to get ready—do whatever it is you need to do to change your negative behavior.

It's also much tougher to bounce back from a repeat offense. She won't believe that you're truly sorry if you do the same thing over and over. Your credibility will be shot, and once you've lost that, your relationship will be the next thing to go. The goal is to show her that your mistake was a one-time indiscretion, not a persistent character flaw.

In addition to the points mentioned above, keep in mind that time is of the essence. After an explosion, you have to act rapidly to limit the fallout. Don't give her the time to mull over your error and become increasingly angry. Taking your sweet time before putting the relationship recovery techniques into action also gives her a chance to consult with her girlfriends, which is never good. (They will usually side with her and encourage her to go tough on you.)

So admit you messed up immediately and, with sincerity, make it up to her, then move on from your mistake.

IS IT TIME FOR A RELATIONSHIP BREAK?

Arguments and ruptures in relationships aren't always precursors to make-ups or resolutions. Sometimes a dispute emerges out of a transgression that you might find difficult to forgive, or proves to be symptomatic of a deeper, more serious issue. In these instances, you may find yourself considering the option of taking a breather from your woman.

While some (read: the girlfriend) may think that spending time apart is an extreme measure, it might be just what the doctor ordered. Whether you want to keep your options open or send her a sign that she needs to change her attitude, this space could be the thing to make or break the relationship.

Reasons for the break

The reasons for needing or wanting a break are diverse and could affect guys differently depending on the level of commitment and communication already established with their ladies.

Here are some of the most common:

■ **Things are moving too fast (or too slow)**

She may be pressuring you to commit way too soon. Conversely, you may be waiting for her to show signs that she's as into you as you are her. Either way, your speeds are mismatched, and the longer you wait, the more apparent it becomes.

■ **Things are getting stale**

The same old routine, day in and day out, has you going stir-crazy. She refuses to change her patterns or try anything new with you. This can seriously cramp your style and may make you reconsider how much longer you can actually take her. If you can't enjoy each other's hobbies or passions and explore new ones together, it may be time for some breathing space.

■ **You think you've fallen out of love (or "like")**

It happens. For some reason, the magic or chemistry you initially experienced fades after the "honeymoon" phase, and you no longer have the same feelings for her. To put it simply, you don't think about her when she's not around, and you could probably go days without getting together with her.

■ She no longer respects you

No matter what you say or do, she just doesn't listen to or respect your opinions anymore. This would be tough for anyone to stomach, but think about why this could have happened: Have you changed? Has your ambition disappeared? Think about this one hard before requesting time apart.

■ She takes you for granted

Have you been her doormat lately? Think about whether there's been a serious imbalance of compromises or chores—a break could be the wake-up call she needs to realize just what she has.

■ You feel smothered

She clings to you everywhere you go. Friends can't see you alone, your phone time is interrupted by her, and you can't even enjoy "alone time" by yourself anymore because she simply doesn't give you space. So give yourself some and at the same time, let her know you need this for your sanity's sake.

■ You're not sexually compatible

Rough, very rough. That's how you like it, and she absolutely wants nothing to do with it. Or perhaps you enjoy nice ol' vanilla sex and she just keeps slicing your back open with her fingernails every time you do it. Whatever the specific incompatibility, this is huge. Sex is an integral part of any relationship, and if you can't enjoy it or if she's not receptive to talking about it, do some re-evaluating.

■ You want to see what else is out there

You simply may not be ready to settle for one woman yet. Maybe you need to see other people to re-invigorate waning confidence in yourself. Or maybe you're questioning whether she's "The One." The only way to know for sure might be to experience other women and find out (the hard way, mind you) just what you had with her.

Expect various reactions

Keep in mind that suggesting a break is taken more seriously when you're not fighting. Furthermore, you must be aware that taking a break, or even bringing it up, can cause irreparable harm to your relationship. So don't make such a decision in the heat of the moment.

That said, asking for a break is no easy task. If your woman has no idea this is coming, chances are she won't take it well, so it's a good idea to prepare for a vast array of emotional reactions.

These include:

■ **She wants to talk about it.** Indulge her; maybe she didn't know how you felt and things can still be salvaged . . . together. But remind her (if applicable) that you have already tried to talk to her, and her indifference led you to this drastic measure.

■ **She throws a tantrum/cries.** Remember to stay calm. She hasn't had the same amount of time to think about this. Even if you both know that something is wrong with your relationship, the fact that you want a break is news to her and could spark quite the outburst of indignation and flying dinnerware.

■ **If you live together, she might throw you out of the house.** Let her. Cool off for a few days and then see how you both feel. Just prepare a suitcase beforehand so she doesn't throw all your stuff out on the lawn.

■ **She gives you the cold shoulder.** She may be internalizing her anger/sadness. She may feel bad, or expect you to try to talk to her. Don't take the bait. This could be a good thing, as she may finally have to think about why you would even want time apart.

Points to establish

Having reassured yourself that your decision to take a break in your relationship is the right one, make sure you discuss all of the following points, for clarity's sake. There's nothing worse than getting your distance at the cost of misinterpreted reasoning and thereby destroying any chance of reconciliation (if that's what you're ultimately aiming for) later on. Ask yourself the following questions before going through with this:

How long will the break be? Think of an appropriate amount of time that you feel will allow you to explore your relationship and why you've taken this measure. Make it clear to her that after this time, you'd like to talk again and see how each of you feels. At this point, you'll know for certain if another go at the relationship would be worthwhile or doomed to fail.

Do you cut all contact? Make sure you mutually agree to the frequency of contact. If there is to be zero contact, lay that on the table. If you think you should still talk once a week to check up on each other, tell her. You may have shared a lot together, and there's no need to keep her up at night, thinking about how you're doing . . . unless, of course, this is exactly why you wanted the break—so that she can realize how much she'll miss you when you're out of reach.

Can you see other people? Depending on the reasons behind the break, you want to be unmistakably clear about this point. You must realize that if you get to sow your wild oats, so does she. If you can handle the thought of her romping around with other men, then by all means, game on. But if you experience any doubts about this liberty while spending time apart, you must address this before parting ways. It's often very difficult to start over once you've crossed this line.

Make the right decision

If you realize that you need a healthy break from your sweetheart, suck it up and tell her. You may lose what you have together, but it might be worth the loss if you needed the break in the first place.

Can a break really do more good than harm? You be the judge. Your situation may warrant the break, but always be mindful of the fact that this is a watershed in your relationship, the fallout from which is never easily determined over the short term.

Be sure to explain to your girlfriend why you need a timeout. She might even rectify the problem without your having to take the actual break. And wouldn't that be a nice break?

6 BREAKUP TIPS FOR A BROKEN RELATIONSHIP

Relationships often go bad—and stay that way. Even when both people know that they would be happier with someone else, it's human nature to procrastinate about difficult decisions. Rather than riding inertia's wave, use these seven helpful tips to break up and move on.

1. Make her the first to know

Out of respect for your girlfriend, never tell your friends you're going to break up before telling her it's over. The all-too-connected grapevine is not the place she should hear that you're no longer interested.

2. Find a neutral zone

It's not a good idea to end the relationship at your place, nor should you be forced to see a picture of you and her hugging on her fridge. Try to find a neutral space where both of you would be comfortable to express your feelings, like a park.

3. End it in person

Be courteous and tell her face-to-face. Phone calls and e-mail are fine for small talk, but this is a big issue.

4. Keep it simple

There's no need to put her through the history of your decision to break up. She does deserve an explanation, but save her (and yourself) the long-winded explanations of exactly why and how things went sour.

5. Don't change your mind

She may argue, cry, or even "not understand why you're doing this," but be sure and stick to your guns. There's nothing worse than a flip-flop relationship—you're either in or out.

6. Be ready for tears

Ending a relationship can evoke intense feelings, and she's not about to save you from seeing them all pour out at once. When she does start to cry, be sympathetic, but don't be drawn in by an overflow of powerful emotion.

TOP 10 WAYS TO GET HER BACK

What if you have made a mistake: You have broken up with a girl and now you want her back? Or, what if you have been kicked to the curb and you want to change your beloved's mind? These pearls of wisdom will help you win her heart back.

10. Reach out and touch her

Yes, it sounds simple, but it is a cardinal sin to play too hard to get when the girl showed you the door, or vice versa, in the first place. The fact that she would text-message you ten times a day when you were together does not mean that she will call you once a week now that you're apart. She is probably somewhat shy and has men courting her anyway.

9. E-mail her

This is not to say that you should send her love poems in red text, but you can forward her an interesting article, a picture, even a simple note saying, "hey, what's up?"

8. Don't "frequent" other girls

Sure, it's tempting. She might understand if you date another girl, maybe even if you kiss her after the date. But if you want her back, don't go any further.

7. Don't ever forget birthdays or anniversaries

You are neither Brad Pitt nor James Dean, so don't play Joe Cool and hurt her forever by forgetting to call on her birthday. Every girl wants to be the center of the universe and treated like a princess, especially on her birthday. If you can, send her a card. If you can't, send her an e-card.

6. Call her every now and then

Again, uncertainty is to be avoided in life, finance, and love. She'd rather know what you are up to than imagine you are with another woman. Comfort her by showing you care, that she's still in your thoughts, and that she always will be.

5. Analyze and study her

Be careful and attentive when she speaks. You are no longer sleeping with her, and increasingly, a facade is being built between the two of you. So read deep into what she says to you, and what she doesn't.

4. Don't be jealous; be on the lookout

The best way to see how she feels about you after a breakup, and what your chances of getting back together are, is to see how she acts with other guys. Does she stand up for you when they put you down? Or does she take out the butcher knife and dig it into your back? Does she see her male friends to talk about the breakup, or is she making out with them in the car? You won't be told directly, but hints are there for the taking.

3. Don't play games

It's hard. It's always recommended that you be somewhat reserved. But that is one thing, and playing games is a totally different ballgame. Signals are very important. As a result, you are better off emitting the correct signals to make the transition. Don't play with her; you don't want to mess her up for life.

2. Hold your cards to your chest

The previous point still stands, but nonetheless, keep your cards close. Why? Relationships are hard enough when you are together. But the real factor is power. Power is key in business just as it is in love. Give her too much power by saying those three words and you'll be whipped faster than you can say "boo."

1. Stay in shape and improve yourself

No matter who initiated the split, there were reasons for the breakup. Make sure that you always hold your head up high and improve on the things that she complained about. Why? You want her to regret her decision, right? What better way than to live life to the fullest and show her that you did everything that she said you would never do? That applies to love, life, and business.

RULE 8
IMPRESS HER FAMILY

For us men, one of the first milestones in a romantic relationship is meeting the woman's family. It's a moment to be welcomed, as it indicates that she is open to the idea of you one day joining her clan. It's also a moment to be apprehensive about, as it will play a part in determining whether or not they will ultimately accept you.

Despite the weight that you attach to meeting her family, however, the event itself will likely not have much in the way of dressing or decoration. Typically, such first meetings occur at casual, low-key events—family barbecues or reunions, for example. But that's not to say that you shouldn't be prepared. And preparing you is the goal of the present chapter.

IMPRESS HER SIBLINGS

Your first foray into her family life will most likely be a meeting with her siblings rather than her parents. Whatever you do, don't discount the sibling opinion in the dating world. While mom and dad *are* important to win over, siblings are often close in age and in personality and can be tougher to fool. Impressing them is not only difficult, it's important: Her brothers and sisters are likely to play a role in any eventual parental-approval process, either talking you up or talking you down as they see fit.

The basics apply when you meet anyone you're trying to impress, so it's best to do some research before diving in. Ask your girlfriend for details on basic family dynamics, their sense of humor, their professions, and their hobbies. Because your lack of familiarity with marine biology or professional bowling is understandable, do a little research if things are foreign to you. Not only will it impress your girlfriend that you've taken such an interest, but it will also make your initial conversation flow more smoothly if you don't have to ask dumb questions about her sister's job or brother's hobby.

Your action plan for that first meeting still needs to be fine tuned depending on whether you're meeting her brother or her sister—each has a different set of things that are going to impress or annoy them. Read on for a few tips on how to ace that first meet and greet.

Win over her sister

Charm her

You managed to land a girlfriend, so one would assume you know a little about charming the ladies, and those skills are going to come in handy when you meet your girlfriend's sister. The key is to combine that winning charm with your best job interview manner to ensure you don't flirt and come off looking like you're hitting on her. Keep your comments and conversation light, yet flattering.

Obviously, you won't be able to steer clear of first-date-type topics like her job or last vacation, but you do have to avoid typical date-like answers. Put away your carefully practiced answers and try to act like you're talking to someone from the office instead. Remember, you aren't trying to impress her as a woman; you just want to impress her as a person. Keep asking questions and make sure you involve both your girlfriend and her sister at all times to avoid any accusations of flirting.

Dig a little

One of the best things about meeting her family—really, one of the only good things—is the opportunity to dig for dirt on your girl. Sisters have all the gossip on formative years and possibly also on current states of mind. Ease into asking questions about your girlfriend and what she was like growing up, and let Sis direct the type of stories that are appropriate to be shared. She'll be impressed that you want to know more about their collective childhood, and she'll relax telling familiar stories.

Women are well aware that this optional story time isn't for everyone, so by asking these questions, you signal your intent to be a suitor rather than just a casual date, which is one of the main things the sister will want to know. And yes, you are allowed to laugh if the anecdotes are exceptionally funny or embarrassing, but don't stoop to making fun of your girlfriend or you could risk looking like a traitor.

Dress well

You never have a second chance to make a first impression. Any impression you make in the first few minutes can be crucial, considering women are known for sizing up men quickly, concisely, and, in their minds, accurately. Your initial impression is multifaceted, so you need to put thought into your appearance, not just your conversation. Humans are visual creatures, and you'll want to display that you are well-kept and suitable rather than dirty and slovenly.

What you wear also gives you a great opportunity to express yourself and let your personality shine, so throw on clothes that both look good and give a little insight into what you're all about. This helps give a quick idea about the kind of guy you are and can even be a point of conversation. For example, wearing a great jacket you picked up the last time you were in New York can be a great conversation point if you get stuck for something to say later on in the meet and greet.

Share details

If you've been dating your girlfriend for more than a week, you've likely noticed a few quirks and peculiarities. Some might drive you crazy and others might just make you laugh. Sisters are great people to share those little tidbits with, since she can possibly confirm that you aren't imagining these things.

Let's say you've noticed that your girlfriend always watches horror movies with her eyes closed or avoids eating foods that are purple; her sister might have insight into the whys of her quirks and she might also have a few good ones for you to keep an eye out for in the future. You'll win points here by looking like you're paying attention to your girlfriend and by noticing what stands out about her, neither of which are bad ideas.

Divide and conquer

Sisters are often competitive, and the last thing you want to do is spark jealousy by focusing too much on one or the other. Since you spend lots of time with your girlfriend, and not so much with her sister, make sure to treat your new friend as a separate entity and not just like a third wheel on your date.

Ask questions that don't focus solely on your girlfriend; she might be sensitive if her sister has always been the center of attention and that might be enough to leave her with a bad taste in her mouth. Ask about her job or an accomplishment that she is proud of; she'll be doubly impressed that you asked and that her sister told you about it.

Win over her brother

Sincere common ground

Any time you find yourself having a conversation with another guy for the first time, it's common for talk to fall into some pretty broad categories:

sports, cars, work, hobbies, and women. Obviously, you'll be avoiding the topic of women, so you'll need to find other subjects to spark her brother's interest. That advance research should help give you hints about what her brother does and how he spends his time, which will then give you clues as to what will get him talking.

It's best not to try to feign interest in a topic that bores you to death or that you are completely clueless about, unless you're an Oscar-worthy actor—you may end up with a brother-in-law who loves that you're *so* into muscle cars, and you're bound to get busted eventually.

Keep it clean

As mentioned above, conversations with her brother will be devoid of all talk of women and sex. If you are going to talk about your girlfriend, avoid anything that could suggest that she has any knowledge of carnal activities at all. It might seem obvious, but if you feel pressured for things to say or alcohol is involved, you might trick yourself into thinking that the guy code transcends the fact that you're dating his sister. It doesn't. He doesn't want to hear it, and you definitely don't want him to think that you would talk that way in front of or about his sister.

Ditto for dirty jokes and suggestive comments: Risqué movies or magazines, strip clubs, sleepovers at your place, or how your girlfriend can't function in the morning without a pre-coffee romp are all off limits. A brother doesn't want to be able to associate you with anything inappropriate for his wholesomely PG sister and the lifestyle he prefers to imagine her having—remember that a brother is just a step below a father, and you wouldn't be sharing your bedroom tales with daddy.

Brotherly protector

Brothers are protective and tend to take their sister's safety quite seriously. Some of the main things he'll be sizing up are whether or not you look trustworthy, sane, loyal, and protective. He wants to know that someone is looking out for his sis and is capable of treating her well, especially if he isn't around to do it himself.

You'll want to be subtle about it; there's no need to make up wild stories of 1 a.m. alley brawls in defense of her honor, but you need to portray those qualities somehow to get a seal of approval. His endorsement is impossible if he hears stories of bad behavior, disrespect, or debauchery. Even if it was as simple as taking a look at her busted stereo or not letting her walk alone late at night, let him know about it, because if he feels like his sister's basic safety needs are being met, he'll be able to relax.

Home court advantage

One of the most-believed superstitions in sports is that of the home court advantage—and it isn't all fallacy. The mental edge gained from familiar surroundings can be enough to boost a player beyond normal limits. It might seem counterproductive, but the best move is to suggest meeting up at place that is familiar turf for her brother rather than for you and voluntarily give up your home court advantage.

Letting him choose the venue or the activity will make him feel in charge, more comfortable, and less threatened. The subliminal message you send when you offer up home court advantage in a situation where most would want it is one of self confidence and ease—her brother is sure to see that as a good thing.

Familiarly unfamiliar

The last thing to keep in mind is that you aren't there to make a new drinking buddy. You're being introduced for two reasons only: So her family can meet the man she is dating, and so that you can meet those who are important to her. Just because you're close to your girlfriend and feel like you can talk about anything, it doesn't mean that feeling should extend to her family right off the bat, especially not to her brother.

Even if there is going to be a friendship between the two of you in the future, it won't be automatic, so remember that you aren't his buddy yet. With that in mind, keep conversation topics general and non-confrontational to make sure you don't insinuate familiarity that hasn't yet been built. He's bound to get his back up if he feels you've overstepped the boundaries, so avoid talking money, sex, politics, and religion during your first get-together at all costs. There's no sense in alienating him right away by putting him under the microscope.

A family affair

Meeting family members can be pretty stressful and is much more important than impressing her friends. Making a good first impression can mean the difference between chilly family dinners and warm holiday receptions, so make sure you do it right. Her brothers and sisters can prove to be a tricky bunch. They may feel like your peers, but they are most definitely not to be treated as such, at least not in the beginning.

A GUIDE TO MEETING HER PARENTS

No two sets of parents are entirely alike, but they do share common goals: protecting their little girl and making it difficult for you—the alien interloper—to achieve your goal of winning them over. All parents want what's best for their daughter, so your very first step is to treat your lady as if she is the most important thing in your world. Their initial impression of you comes directly from her, so never give her a reason to trash you.

In all you do, follow the screenwriter's mantra: show, don't tell. If your value is effectively displayed, most people don't need to be told anything. Her parents have endured the phony prattle of boastful men before you; they want to see for themselves what makes you perfect for their daughter. Thus, let your actions represent you.

Finally, we tend to treat couples married for many years as a unit, yet a key to winning over her parents lies in building independent relationships with each of them. This is especially true if her parents are divorced.

First impressions

Show discretion and confidence

Prior to meeting her parents, have your girlfriend prep you on areas of common interest and taboo topics; it's on you to exploit whatever ground you may share. Avoid emotional or highly charged issues; reserve your strong opinions for when you know them better.

If necessary, arm yourself with assured answers to the kinds of questions a parent might ask, such as "Where do you see yourself in five years?" No, this is not a job interview; in fact, some would say that the stakes are much higher.

Show respect and restraint

Strictly speaking, keep your manners on full display: treat her folks with the utmost respect when you're around them, and when not, speak well of them. When they come to your door, be there to greet them and welcome them in. At their place, get up and do the dishes after dinner and make sure to go easy on the liquor. Last, but not least, until they tell you otherwise, they're Mr. and Mrs. Girlfriend to you.

Show initiative and interest

Make the first move and invite them to dinner at your place. You can stress the importance of this meeting by making it formal. Either way, it's a great chance to show them your financial situation, interests, lifestyle, or your ability to cook and keep a nice place, without having to say a word.

At their place, ask to be guided through family photo albums. Showing a genuine interest in your girl's family and a clear interest in her history can work in your favor. She's her parents' pride and joy; they love to show her off and relate the details of her childhood.

What to bring

Chances are you'll eventually be invited to the lady's parents' house for dinner. Even if it's not exactly Thanksgiving dinner, you shouldn't come to a family's house empty-handed if you're an invited guest.

Whatever the occasion, the safest thing to bring is a nice floral arrangement. A bottle of wine or a box of chocolates is also acceptable, but perhaps you should ask your girlfriend first, in case her father is a recovering alcoholic or her mother is on a strict diet.

Show creativity and attention

Eschew the obvious flowers and bring a few photos of you and your girlfriend having a good time together to your first parental meeting. Pictures act as brilliant conversation starters, and they can help drive home your compatibility—always a key to winning them over.

On that note, provided your first meeting with them is along the lines of dinner or another event, bring a camera. This suggests you regard the evening as significant solely because you are meeting them and you want to preserve it in a picture.

What to say

This is where your small-talk skills come in handy; use them. Unless you have a tendency to feel comfortable with people immediately, it's normal to be at a loss for conversation topics with the parents of your newest ladylove. You don't want to say the wrong thing or come across as a blabbermouth, but you also don't want to appear like a lump on a log—useless, with absolutely nothing to say.

So what do you talk about?

It's always good to ask a lot of questions and show interest in their family life. For example, refer to something your girlfriend told you and say, "Tamara told me you shot a hole-in-one today, did you have to buy the whole club free drinks?" Look for any common ground you share with the father or mother, such as similar hobbies and interests, a love for the same sports team, or a passion for dogs, and work from there.

If it's the first time you're meeting them, they will likely have a list of questions for you. Don't panic, they just want to get to know the man their daughter has fallen for. Answer the questions politely, and try to relate them back to her parents.

Suggested topics:

- your job

- your family

- sports

- movies (recent or old)

- pets (if they own any)

Stay away from:

- jokes (until you know their sense of humor)

- politics

- personal questions

- religion

- money or income

- sex

Be prepared

Would you go to a job interview for AT&T without knowing what AT&T stood for?

You should have the same attitude regarding meeting your girlfriend's parents; you need to do some research.

This means asking your girlfriend what you should know about her parents and family, including what line of work they are or were in, whether they're serious or have a sense of humor, and whether they prefer people who are outgoing or more reserved.

You should also ask your girlfriend for the important tidbits concerning her family situation, like if her parents are remarried, if either of her parents has another child, and whether or not her grandparents are still alive.

If you've been with your girlfriend for a while and are making the transition to the serious stage, then chances are you'll already know the essential information, but it's always better to get the whole scoop and be aware of her entire family situation.

There's no need to illustrate the disaster that could occur if her father is a former Marines general, and you tell him you don't care to defend your country in war, or if you refer to her bodacious stepmother as the father's daughter.

Asking your girlfriend questions about her family will also help you score points with her, as it will show her that you care to make the necessary effort with her family and that you're interested in her family life.

Her father

A woman's father sees himself as her armor, and he has reason to be on guard. After all, he was once just like you: green and deluded by his own cleverness in aiming to defile another daddy's little girl. But today he has one thing you don't: the realization that those fathers knew his moves and motives, just like he knows yours. He will protect his little girl at all costs, and until you can win him over, you aren't his friend.

Seek ways to connect with him man to man. Naturally, you shouldn't propose scoring lap dances at a strip club, but you should strive for him to identify you as a respectable member of the male clan. Until you can show him who you are independent of his daughter, he may always regard you with suspicion and treat you as a threat.

Her mother

Never underestimate her influence: In your girlfriend's mother, you face your toughest and potentially most vocal critic. Her principal image of you, built on words from her daughter, is far too complete for comfort. You stand little chance against it, since she can't possibly see all the reasons your girl's crazy about you. It's your job to show her.

Forget the flawed notion of looking at a girl's mother to see the girl in twenty years. Instead, imagine that the mother is looking at her daughter and seeing herself twenty years ago. She wants to see that girl madly in love, ecstatically happy, and treated like the royalty her daughter surely is.

In this light, you will want to relate to your lady's mother on two levels. Most of the time, she is a mature parent and your elder, and to this woman you show courtesy and respect bordering on genuflection. But she's also that girl from twenty years ago: wickedly fun and flirty, and forever receptive to the attention of a charming man. Work to draw one solid, respectful line in the sand while simultaneously stretching a foot forward to blur another. Let the playful accusations of a harmless crush going in either direction roll right off your back.

Identify your allies

It's a given that you want your girlfriend's parents to tell her what a good catch you are. Your aim is to get along with both parents and to get on their good sides, but here's a little secret: Her mother is also your ally.

This depends on who your girlfriend is closer to—her mother or her father—but her mother is really the one who holds the power. She's the one who will invite you over for dinner, she's the one who will defend you if you ever get on her father's bad side, and she's the one who will stick up for you if your girlfriend is crying over what a jerk you are.

Fathers will always have a harder time accepting you; you're the man in her life now (at least, that's how he looks at it), and she'll go to you with her problems rather than to her pops. Dad will always be an obstacle, but if tackled properly, you can get on his good side.

Here's the clincher: You don't want to become best friends with her dad, unless your girlfriend is really close to her father. Get on her dad's good side, but don't go on fishing trips with him, don't have inside jokes with him about your girlfriend, and refrain from discussing legal papers all night if you're both lawyers. In her eyes, you don't want to seem like a guy who would be her dad's best friend if you were the same age. You want to be considered the son he never had.

Win them over

Get some help from your girl, trust yourself and your instincts, and dive in. You can do only so much to win over her parents, and you should do only so much; beyond that, it's out of your hands. At least your girl will appreciate your efforts, especially when it comes time to meet *your* parents.

You'll get there

As long as you're animated, personable, polite, know what to say, and show respect for your girlfriend, her parents will love you.

They surely want the best for their little girl, so if your girlfriend has nothing but great things to say about you, and you prove your worthiness with good manners and a genuine interest in her family, they will accept you with open arms.

TOP 10 WAYS TO IMPRESS HER MOM

Let's look at some specific steps you can take toward impressing her parents, beginning with the real power-player: Mom. With time, any man can win over the mother of the woman he falls in love with. Just remember these ten tips to earn points when you encounter a woman's mother those precious first few times.

Number 10: Listen to her

This is a very obvious one, yet it is so often forgotten. Mothers are wise and experienced enough to merit your attention when they are speaking. So when it comes to making a first impression, be courteous enough to shut up and listen to what your lady's mom has to say.

Number 9: Be yourself

With age and experience comes an unparalleled knack for picking out phonies, and if you are not being yourself with her mother, she will sense it and suspect that you are also less than forthright with her daughter. Just be yourself and, most of all, be sincere in everything you do.

Number 8: Compliment her

If she is sixty-five years old but looks like she's pushing eighty, don't insult her intelligence by asking what she'll be doing for her fiftieth birthday. Be sincere, or at least sound it, by flattering her on something that you've been afforded insight on: her cooking, her hospitality, or interesting family anecdotes.

Number 7: Remember important dates

It never hurts to call her and wish her a happy birthday. Doing so shows that you respect and care about the woman who brought your woman into this world.

Number 6: Positive presentation

If you show up looking unshaven and are dressed like you're headed for the unemployment line, chances are that mom will not be impressed. In fact, she may even be offended by your lack of etiquette.

Number 5: Offer your services

If you can ever offer to help her around the house by clearing dishes or even give her a ride somewhere, you will earn many points. Actions such as these imply selflessness and thoughtfulness, two very important traits for mothers.

Number 4: Never disrespect her daughter

It sounds obvious, but you must never disrespect her daughter in front of her, particularly during the early stages. Down the road, teasing your woman in a friendly, playful manner can be acceptable, especially if you've built a good rapport with her mother.

Number 3: Take Mom's side

The idea here isn't to ditch your girlfriend and defend her mother, but rather to demonstrate to both that you're an independent-minded man with a fair sense of values. Don't be too eager to do so and barge in with an opinion where it's not welcome; in fact, you're best off waiting for an explicit invitation to weigh in on a debate or dispute that they're having. When the occasion arises, play the diplomatic role and explain to one why the other views things differently. You may get some shelling in the short term, but you will surely be awarded a medal of honor in the long run.

Number 2: Make her daughter's dreams come true

Every mother hopes for the happiness of her daughter and hopes that she will lead a better life than her own. Without showing off or going overboard about it, take the steps that you can to make your woman's aspirations—personal, professional, and romantic—come true.

Number 1: Love her daughter

At the end of the day, no amount of gifts, trips, or compliments can come close to the love and affection you offer a woman. That is all her mother will want.

TOP 10 WAYS TO WIN OVER HER FATHER

Unlike her mother, Dad doesn't give a damn about dates, you'll be lucky if he's even pretending to listen to you, and sure, he wants his daughter's dreams to come true—just not with you . . . at least, not at this stage.

While the two share some basic goals, winning over her father presents a substantially different challenge.

Keep in mind that men are, by nature, visual. Your girlfriend can tell her father about all your winning attributes but, trusting his own judgment, he needs to witness them for himself. Remember, let your general mantra be to *show*, not tell.

Number 10: Turn down the PDA

Not your Blackberry (although you should silence all such technology), but your public displays of affection. Mom might want to see a certain level of intimacy, but at this stage, Dad likely does not.

The key is to express your affection for his daughter with tact and subtlety. A reasonable rule of thumb: keep whatever displays you show to small, quick gestures. Around the house, put your modesty on display. Light hand-holding is acceptable, and if she's eager to drape her arm around you, fine, don't shirk from it, but keep things to a kiss on the cheek or a short rub on her shoulder.

Number 9: Respect your roles

Be casual and try to talk to him as another man, but maintain a respectful distance—don't be too casual.

As a general—if unspoken—rule, men don't open up to one another the way women might, so don't be over-anxious to spread the good word about him, yourself, or his daughter. If you allow your roles with respect to one another to develop organically, your relationship with her dad stands a much better chance of thriving down the road.

Number 8: Find out his interests beforehand

Don't just be a suck-up; rather, seek interests around which the two of you can build conversation and common-interest bonds.

Don't rely on male stereotypes—sports, cars, etc.—for conversation. Once you've learned about his interests, whether from your girl or directly from him, follow up on them in your next meeting by bringing a germane magazine article that you think he might find interesting.

Number 7: Bring him a manly gift

Cater this gift to his personality and deliver it with as much cool indifference as you can muster. Ideally this gift should be something the two of you can share together, for example, out on the porch or in an otherwise mellow moment.

You might consider beer (does he drink domestic, microbrews, imports?), wine (red or white?), smoked meats, or a sports DVD. Whatever the gift, keep it all cool. Taking this step exposes you to a harrowing precipice or two: The right gift gets you in. The wrong one—you're an ass-kisser.

Number 6: Ask him about himself

Give the man a platform for the stories he loves to tell. Let the rest of the family roll their eyes at a narrative they've heard a hundred times. You're a fresh audience—a storyteller's delight.

As your base, go with something your girl has told you about before, but keep away from inappropriate content—that is, the drunken college stories. Rather, think sports, professional life, or even pranks you've heard about.

Number 5: Always be a gentleman

The purpose of proper etiquette is not to make you look like a snobby master of manners but to allow social interactions to run smoothly, and the absence of etiquette makes you realize how important it really is.

Without making a spectacle, carry out the small details as though they're part of your disposition: Exhibit the kinds of good manners that make up the unspoken male vernacular. Look Dad in the eye, shake his hand when you see him, and greet his wife according to how she greets you—that is, with a handshake or a hug.

Number 4: Ask for his advice

Appeal to his experience. Fathers—men in general—enjoy offering their advice or opinion, and provided you don't overdo it, he'll feel he still has some influence in his daughter's life, albeit indirectly.

Keep your initial appeal somewhat impersonal. For example, general career advice or moderate family issues are reasonable starting points. But asking him for advice on what to do about an arrest warrant or genital warts? Don't go there.

Number 3: Be mature

Neither join him nor lead him in a descent into guy immaturity; we all may share certain frat-boy weaknesses, but this isn't the time to remind anyone of this.

Your goal should be a flexible maturity, one that takes the quiet, dignified road with regard to farts, burps, "playful" disrespect to women, excessive interest in the game on TV, or any behavior that would mortify your own mother if she were around to witness it.

Although "be yourself" is the only reliable motto, if you're a degenerate frat boy, you might want to suppress those impulses for the time being. The point is to win over Dad without selling your soul, but you can do that without descending into a primal state.

Number 2: Show some old-school values

This is fairly fundamental: Be a stand-up guy, not just because the alternative makes you look like a weasel but because he'll have no choice but to respect it. He can find plenty of weak reasons to dislike you, but he can't hold your being a man of values against you.

If an issue needs to be addressed—anything from misunderstandings to missed appointments to owning up to the truth in whatever capacity—address it like a man.

Number 1: Showcase your reliability

At some point, her dad has to let go of his little girl, and you want to be there when he does. Respond to that deep-seated paternal need to know he can depend on you to take care of her when he does let go.

So be on time to anything that concerns him; dinner at the folks' house or dinner out, or any sort of get-together. Give the appearance of financial stability. Maintain the safety and reliability of your car. And be there—wherever "there" might be—when his daughter needs you.

Deal with her dad

While every father is different, they retain a common goal: to defend their daughters from the likes of their former selves. To that end, they already believe they know you—or at least some of your motives—very well.

Overcoming these intrinsic preconceptions may prove to be your toughest obstacle, but if you've come this far, the girl is surely worth the effort.

RULE 9
MAKE THE COHABITATION LEAP

With the milestone of meeting the parents successfully behind you, the next, more dramatic one isn't far down the road. With your woman feeling secure and confident in her relationship with you, she may start applying the squeeze for the two of you to take the next step together: moving in.

Is it always the woman who initiates this proposal? Clearly not, but with men being the independent creatures that we are, it oftentimes is her idea. Unfortunately, that doesn't take any pressure off of you to make what is a tough decision. In approaching it, time is your ally; get it on your side by anticipating her raising the issue if you don't plan to do so yourself.

5 SIGNS SHE WANTS TO MOVE IN WITH YOU

Some of your friends are probably already living with their girlfriends, but is your woman interested in living with you? Watch for signs that she's thinking about this next step so that you can decide—before the big talk—if you're ready.

1. She decorates your place

Watch out if your girlfriend starts changing the décor in your bachelor pad. Recognize that decorating and even cleaning make her feel more attached to your place. The new tablecloth in the dining room that she picked out gives her a sense of belonging. And the matching towels in the bathroom make her feel like she's at home when she steps out of the shower.

It may be tempting to ignore the significance of these small changes. After all, if she has a flair for color and style, then you might even like the new look. But keep in mind that there may be expectations attached.

2. She takes the "y" out of "yours"

Listen to her when she talks about everyday things around your place. Listen carefully. Does she mention that "our" new curtains look good with the furniture, even though you bought them? Or that "our" fridge is set too cold? Language is a window into the mind, and these little signs should tip you off that she wants to blur the line between "your" place and "our" place.

Put the pieces together and start keeping track of what she says. Be sure to pay attention if she starts mentioning how much easier it is for her to commute to work from your apartment, or if she complains about how expensive it is for her to pay rent. Saving money and time are both classic reasons for couples to consider living together. Stay alert and notice them if they start coming up in conversation.

3. She gives out your home phone number

Do you find yourself skipping through messages on your land line's voice mail to get to those that have been left for you? If she's giving your number out to her friends, especially if she hasn't talked to you about it, then you should take notice. By having people call for her, she is planting the seeds of togetherness in your mind. Passing out your number is not just a matter of convenience; it can also be a way of getting (more than just) her foot in the door.

Furthermore, if she actually answers your phone, then you might as well start giving her some closet space.

4. She turns a night into a week

It's become normal for her to sleep over every now and then. When she starts to linger for a few days, whether it's for convenience or pleasure, it may be a signal that she is thinking about a more permanent move. What better way to make you comfortable with the idea?

These extended visits are like training wheels for the real thing, and she might be trying to see if you would make a good roommate. Also notice if she stays at your place when you're away on business trips or out with your buddies on the weekend. This may be her way of checking up on you.

5. She colonizes your space

If a woman is thinking about moving in, she may try to ease you into little details of her lifestyle so that you won't go into culture shock. Having a few of her "basics" in the fridge can be one of her first steps. Once you reach past the soy milk for a beer a few times, you may start to feel like you're losing ground in your own apartment.

Keep an eye on the bathroom, too. A toothbrush is a pretty neutral message (if she sleeps over, you'll be grateful for that in the morning), but stocking the medicine cabinet with sanitary pads is a much stronger one.

Make a decision

If you've seen all or some of these clues that she wants to live with you, it's time to make a decision—or at least start thinking about one. Once you recognize the signs that she wants to move in, you can prepare yourself for the conversation. Let's get you started on deciding whether or not you're ready for this next step.

MOVING IN TOGETHER

Relationships are made up of a continuous number of tests that reveal whether or not two people are indeed right for each other. And one of those tests is undoubtedly that of moving in together.

There are always a few pointers to keep in mind when deciding to dive into the "living as though we're married" relationship. This step in the relationship can make or break a couple looking for its identity. Moving in with a girlfriend is a very big step and involves a lot of responsibility, commitment, disclosure, and compromise. Are you ready for it?

Why move in?

If you're going to move in with that someone special, it's important that you do so for the right reasons. Make sure it is because you want to take the relationship to the next level of commitment, and not because you'll get an easy booty call while you save a little extra money on rent.

When asking yourself if you're ready to pack up and settle down under the same roof as her, you'll want to look at the three basic components of this venture: the bad, the good, and the avoidable.

The bad

Oftentimes, a man and woman may decide to settle in together because they see it as the natural next step in their relationship. But the problem is that they may not be ready for it. Only when it's too late will the couple be able to realize that they moved too fast.

The important thing to remember is that when you and your lover cohabitate, you will ultimately see all the aspects of her personal life—not just the pretty side—when you are together.

You will be privy to all of her behavioral ups and downs, day in and day out. How would you react if she walked around the house with no underwear on? Although your initial reaction may be to jump for joy, think again: Is this the sight you want to be exposed to while you are watching television? Once again, you may think that this sounds delightful, but prolonged exposure has an effect of deadening sex appeal.

Here are just a few of the reasons why you should consider *not* moving in together:

There's no U in WE

By moving in, you have to accept that you no longer get to make decisions on your own. From this point forward, you'll always have to consult with your "better half" before making a final decision. In other words, you'll have to deal with a lot more "red tape."

Where are you going?

Your schedule will no longer be as free or as accommodating (to your needs) as it used to be. You'll need more than a few hours' notice before making plans with your buddies. In fact, don't be surprised if you hear yourself saying, "Well, let me check with Betty beforehand, to see if our schedule is free."

Players can't play

If you're still a player and enjoy the company of other women, then moving in is absolutely the worst decision you can make, for two main reasons:

First, the fact that you still need to see other women proves that you're not ready for a commitment, nor are you satisfied with your current partner.

Second, you'll be making it much harder to go about your player business. That's right, no more "girl friends" for you.

Select company

Your still very single friends will not be as "welcome" around the house as they once were. Your woman knows very well that a single man can be a bad influence on his committed friend. Don't be surprised if, as a result, they no longer invite you out as often as they used to.

Think pink

According to the popularly received (and largely proved) notion that women are better decorators than men, you will have to give in to her annual redecorating needs. Say bye-bye La-Z-Boy, hello pink curtains.

Stinky, dirty boxers

The privileges of leaving your underwear lying around the house and the dishes piled up, and the freedom to fart at your leisure, will all disappear with your new roommate—especially if you still want to keep the sexual attraction alive and well.

That's my HDTV

There are also plenty of legal concerns to be kept in mind, such as who signs the lease (it should be both of you), and who buys and keeps the furniture in case things don't work out.

The good

On the brighter side of things, this step into long-term companionship might actually bring the two of you closer together. This is, at times, the kind of launching pad that can solidify a couple. The man and woman may be fearful of spending every minute of their life with each other, especially if they were used to simply seeing each other every other day, at the most.

But to many couples' surprise, this living situation turns out to be great. You might actually enjoy watching your girlfriend dye her hair and give herself a manicure. For that matter, she might enjoy watching you shave or clip your toenails.

It's the little things that make a relationship last in the long run. Will she be able to care for you on Saturday morning when you wake up sick when she had a whole day of shopping planned with her girlfriends?

The avoidable

The problem with sharing a home with your loved one is that the event might be premature and simply triggered by a coincidental turn of events. A good example might be that both of you were planning to move out of your parents' houses and decided to move in together to share the cost of living.

The main issue here is that couples should move in together as a natural transition in a relationship. Finances should not be the basis of the decision for an important step such as this. The important thing to discern is that you're not moving in together just to save money, but rather, because you love each other and are willing to take the relationship a step further. Saving money just happens to be a by-product of the decision to do this.

The greatest benefit of moving in with a woman is the opportunity to figure out just how compatible the two of you really are.

In fact, with the popularity of divorce in America, people should consider moving in together before marriage. Doing so allows them to discover each other's not-so-obvious habits before making a final commitment of marriage. If, after a year or two together, you haven't found any nasty surprises, then you might consider taking your commitment a step further.

The six-month rule

The six-month rule says that you should never move in with a woman you've known for less than six months.

The reason is very logical: it's just too early to know if you like each other enough, have similar interests, or share the same points of views—especially during the honeymoon phase, when your judgment is clouded. This can be very dangerous, particularly in situations that require financial responsibility, such as signing the lease and buying furniture together.

Once you commit to living together, you can't go back. Taking this step will help you realize that the relationship will either work or fail. If the living arrangements are not ideal, you cannot go backward in the relationship, because you'll both realize that if it did not work when you were living together, then there is no use continuing the relationship.

HOW TO PREPARE

A simple checklist can help the unprepared make the most of moving in together.

Make it your own place

Remember that the furniture and design of the place should involve a joint decision. A boyfriend can't just show up with the latest La-Z-Boy, the same way that his woman shouldn't put her collection of dolls on display for all the guy's buddies to stare at during *Monday Night Football*.

Don't reveal everything at once

The idea here is for both of you to become comfortable with each other at a gradual pace. It is not wise to show your woman all your good and bad qualities at once. This might scare her away or repulse her.

Respect each other's space

Just because the two of you are living under the same roof, it doesn't mean that every second of every minute needs to be spent together.

Find some personal spots that each of you can revert to for some quiet time. This will also help when you need a timeout from each other.

Share the responsibility

Splitting up the chores should be second choice to alternating the tasks, so that both of you get your hands dirty. This will in turn allow both of you to put equal amounts of effort into the whole task of cleaning up.

TOP 10 ROMANTIC THINGS TO DO WHEN LIVING TOGETHER

Relationships are a little like glaciers: Under various pressures, they're always moving and changing, gathering all sorts of debris. But after some time, they move so slowly, it's easy to forget they're moving at all, particularly when you live together. To use a more familiar metaphor, one day your relationship is a wild ride, all loops and corkscrews, and then, out of nowhere, it has mellowed and straightened out. Actually, it's worse than that. It has become stagnant.

Hey, it happens. No sweat. Relationships require management, like anything else in your life that's as big and complex. One way is to inject a little romance. Now, depending on your understanding of the subject, you may have to redefine romance a little. It shouldn't always have a direct purpose; in other words, imagine romance as neither a means nor an end. Try to imagine it as something you do for her simply because you love her, and not necessarily to get sex later. Sounds corny, but it's true.

With all that in mind, the home you share with your lady presents a bunch of romantic opportunities to reignite that stagnating relationship. The following suggestions, grounded in the element of surprise, should get you started. In devising your own, plan what you do around your girl's unique tastes. You know her best, so you would know, for example, that she loves chocolate but is currently on a diet, or that she hates roses. Use your inside information.

Number 10: Hand her a hot towel

While she's in the shower or taking a bath, throw her towel in the dryer for a few minutes. When she gets out, present her with the toasty towel. It's sweet and thoughtful; she'll love you for it.

Number 9: Give her a massage

She comes home from a horrendous day at work; she's exhausted and even a little bad-tempered. So what do you do? Offer to give her a massage. Using aromatherapy oils, focus on her neck and back, the areas that tend to tense up under stress and cause aches and pains. You can set a mood by dimming the lights and lighting candles; this creates a more relaxing and romantic environment.

Number 8: Bring her breakfast in bed

A classic gesture, breakfast in bed is the proverbial "oldie but goodie." Get up early on a Saturday or Sunday morning and prepare breakfast just the way she likes it, with toast, fresh fruit, cinnamon buns, whatever. Then surprise her by serving it to her in bed.

Number 7: Write her romantic notes

The love letter or love note is an amazing thing; little effort is required to write her one, and yet you can express so much. So write her a few creative, unique love notes, and leave them in unexpected places around the house. For example, in the morning, tape one to the bathroom mirror or to the coffee machine.

Number 6: Order in

Order in for dinner and have it waiting for her when she gets home. Produce a romantic setting by recreating a restaurant feel on the dining room table (or in front of a fire, on the patio, or wherever else you think might work), complete with plates, silverware, and cloth napkins. For an extra romantic touch, add candles and a small vase with some flowers. Learn how to set a formal table and surprise her with your impeccable taste.

Number 5: Start a fire

In the winter, get a fire going in the fireplace (if you have one, obviously). Then, set up some pillows and blankets, and uncork a bottle of wine. If you want to take things to the next level, have a romantic dinner sitting in front of that otherwise uneventful fireplace.

Number 4: Pack her lunch for work

Surprise her by making a lunch for her to take to work. It's an opportunity to be both thoughtful and romantic, since you can also slip in a love note or a flower. Furthermore, you can buy an individual slice of cake or pie from a bakery, or pick up some other dessert you know she likes.

Number 3: Show her feet a little TLC

Bad day or not, if she's been running around, her feet are probably sore. Prepare a footbath for her and follow it up with a short foot massage. Then, if it feels right, paint her toenails. It might be best to make that last part spontaneous. If, for example, she's planning to do it herself, you can offer your services. You'll be surprised at how romantic—even erotic—it can be.

Number 2: Make her feel sexy with some lingerie

Lingerie is win-win. Your girl feels sexy and attractive wearing it, and the benefits for you go without saying. So buy her some nice lingerie and lay it out on the bed for her. Don't buy the sluttiest thing you can find; the point is to make her feel good about herself. Think about what she likes, what she'll feel good in, then combine that with your own tastes.

Number 1: Draw her a bath

The bathtub is one of the most romantic household locales. Ensure that it is clean, then draw her a hot bath and add bath beads or bubble bath. If all goes well, she'll invite you to join her.

Up the romance

All these romantic gestures will make your woman happy. If you get rewarded in the process, so much the better, but making those rewards your sole motivation can only lead to disappointment. Just try to do it for her, and see what happens; it will probably come back to you.

THREE FACTORS THAT WILL MAKE LIVING TOGETHER FUN

Agree on responsibilities: You might like to do some chores that she despises, and vice versa. Before moving in together, discuss and agree on the living arrangements and responsibilities.

Compromise: There is no way that two people will agree on everything. Therefore, it is important to know when to compromise. Here's a tip: Always put yourself in the other person's shoes and try to understand her point of view before making a drastic decision.

Build a strong team: United you stand, divided you fall. Remember, you're a team, so keep it strong and support each other. This means that you both have to step up and be there for each other in both good times and bad.

BENEFITS OF A GIRLS' NIGHT OUT

Whether or not your girlfriend ends up moving in with you, maturing relationships tend to be accompanied by increasing exposure to one another. Many couples are easily lulled into relying on each other's company, a dependence which quickly leads to boredom and stagnancy within a relationship.

Most men are instinctively aware of the need to maintain some measure of independence from their partner and to allow her to do the same, but still have some issues with seeing her independence in execution. Supposing that every Friday night, your woman puts on a short, sexy dress, lipstick, and her special perfume that drives you crazy. However, every week, on this night, her efforts are not made for you; they're for a night out with her girlfriends.

Should you complain?

In short: No.

You might think of the girls' night out simply as a concession you have to make in a relationship, but a straightforward cost-benefit analysis shows that the girls' night out is much more than that; it is actually mutually beneficial. This means, most important, that her enjoyment translates into big advantages for you.

And once you grasp the potential payback a girls' night has to offer, you will be so appreciative of the ritual that you might even offer to help her pick out a pair of shoes to match her outfit.

She has a night of freedom

Why this will work in your favor: If you are thoughtful and understanding when she wants to go out with her friends, she will be compelled to be the same when you have your night out. For you, this tacit agreement translates into scores of unrestricted nights out with the guys for drinks, sports matches, or wherever your whims might take you.

And this luxury will be granted to you with no explanation needed, and no objections or criticisms on her part.

She gets to flirt and be flirted with

Why this will work in your favor: Innocently flirting with other men (within reason, of course) will make your woman feel sexy and desirable. While this might initially sound unacceptable to you, remember that most women don't actually want to go home with a man they flirt with in a bar or a club.

Instead, your woman will come home to you. And when she does, her sexual appetite will be revved up, and you will reap the benefits of other men's labor.

She gets her need for venting and gossiping out of her system

Why this will work in your favor: First, the opportunity for a woman to express her feelings to her girlfriends is a natural way of relieving stress; your woman will be more relaxed when she returns home.

Second, you will get a well-deserved reprieve from this kind of chit-chat; in other words, her need to gossip or slander her boss, co-workers, and acquaintances will be fulfilled by someone other than you.

She remembers what it was like to be single

Why this will work in your favor: Being single can be great fun, but it also comes with its share of dating horror stories. If she has friends who are single, a night out with them will remind her of some of the less-than-exciting aspects of being on her own.

Going out with her girlfriends will give her a chance to watch them play the field and see what's out there. But don't let any of this worry you; more likely than not, this will just make her appreciate you even more.

She feels confident that her man trusts her

Why this will work in your favor: For a woman, the fact that her boyfriend trusts her is generally a good indication that she is in a mature, stable relationship. Therefore, if you are relaxed and confident that your woman will be faithful to you, she is more likely to honor your confidence.

This not only means that she is more likely to trust you (remember that jealousy on your part breeds jealousy on hers), but she is also more likely to be loyal. It's a win-win situation for both of you.

Enjoy your free time

Relax and let her head out with the girls every so often. Complaints and jealousy are definitely warranted if she does not return home the same night, comes back smelling of men's cologne, or starts going out alone instead of with the girls. But most likely, your woman just wants an innocent night of fun with her posse.

And the good news is that your laidback attitude will make her feel obligated to provide you with as much freedom to go out and party with the boys when you feel like it.

GETTING AWAY WITH A BOYS' NIGHT OUT

The average dude spends more than forty hours a week at work, with maybe another ten spent working at home.

There's sleeping, which can take up to another forty hours, and then we have to consider all the chores and family-oriented activities. Then, there's the time that she'll want to spend with you, which a relationship-savvy man like yourself now knows is worth spending and will reap rewards in the long run.

In the midst of being so generous with your time, however, it's easy to neglect yourself. Guys need to unwind, to find themselves in the company of other Y-chromosomes, to be themselves and not worry about the consequences. In other words, a man like you needs his regular boys' night out.

Man with a plan

Where you go is your business, but every man knows that the best spots for soaking in one's own testosterone usually involve sports, booze, and chicks—but not necessarily in that order.

What will eventually determine your destination is the level of wildness you're willing to attain. Single guys never have trouble with this one; they can sit in a nightclub with their pants down to their ankles without having to make any excuses. But anyone with a serious (particularly a live-in) girlfriend has some serious decisions to make.

In the end, your level of "craziness" is directly proportional to the despotism of your girl. If she keeps you on a tight leash, chances are you won't be getting lap dances in a limo. On the other hand, sometimes a psycho control freak will drive you to the edge of insanity, and that's when you'll be the wildest.

If, alternatively, your woman is loving, trusting, and understanding, no run-of-the-mill testosterone-fueled fellow in his right mind would do anything to damage the relationship.

Talk to her

Tell her about why you need to go out and party. Relationships are built on communication, and you'll never find a better example of it than in this situation. And while you're on an honesty streak, why not tell her the gist of your evening? Females have a tendency to become insecure about the little things. Do yourself a favor and tell her most of the things you and your buddies will be doing. You can leave the spicy details out if you think no serious damage will ensue.

Yes, boys' night out can be extremely entertaining, but try to keep yourself from doing it too often. Going out more frequently than your girl can brand you a selfish deadbeat. She's most likely working as hard as you are and deserves as many good times as you do. So the moment you're starting to have more fun than her, your stock may plummet. Moderation rules.

Lies aren't always the answer

It's possible that you may not be comfortable with all this sincerity. If you intend to lie about the true nature of your evening, do so very cautiously.

With other guys involved, lies have a very good chance of catching up with you. Your buddy may have a tolerant girlfriend who won't mind hearing about the depravity. But watch your back if she shoots her mouth off to your girl, especially if she's not so broadminded. Don't be reckless; evaluate your chances first.

Keep in mind that talk is cheap and a woman is likely to judge your actions. If she's used to seeing you acting crudely and lewdly toward women or constantly eyeballing the all-night buffet, so to speak, don't be surprised if she goes completely ballistic when you suggest that you might be going out with the boys. Earn her trust and it's guaranteed she won't give you trouble over the next boys' night out.

RULE 10
KEEP YOUR RELATIONSHIP EXCITING

Routine is the enemy of many relationships; the lazy man will allow cycles of regularity to take over the planning for him and extract all spontaneity out of romance in the process. While keeping things fresh and exciting will most often work in your favor (and we'll be exploring avenues for doing just this later in the chapter), there are certain rituals that she'll want you to preserve. The most obvious is the anniversary celebration.

ANNIVERSARIES: HAPPY BIRTHDAY TO US

What day is it?

An important aspect of an anniversary is to remember it, and remember it right. Although this might sound like a given, it rarely is. You might think that the anniversary falls 365 days after the two of you made love, for example, but she might consider it to be the first time you kissed her lips.

Pinpointing the proper date is probably an arduous task and, luckily, it only needs to be done once a year. Imagine finding her the perfect present, only to find yourself two weeks late in giving it to her. Establishing when your relationship officially began can be tricky sometimes.

An easy way to bring up the subject is to subtly ask her what made her realize that you were the man for her. This should help you find out at what point in time she began developing serious feelings for you, thereby helping to pinpoint that specific time when you became a pair.

Let's suppose, however, that you actually get the date of your anniversary right; what do you do now?

What should I get?

So what does spending one year together mean? Does it mean that the two of you get along together? Possibly. Does it mean that you love each other? Likely. Does it mean you will have to get out some cash and "prove" your affection to her? Absolutely.

Instead of buying her a "one-year anniversary" present, why not get her a "thank you" gift for all the good times spent together? The key here is to get something that is meaningful to her. There is no point in investing a month's salary in her gift.

You might be tempted to buy her the typical Valentine's Day gifts like flowers, chocolate, perfume, jewelry, or clothes. Although this might be an easy alternative to the time-consuming task of showing her you actually understand and care for her, it's not recommended.

Girlfriends value the effort and thought involved in buying their gift more than the gift itself. This again goes to show that it is not compulsory to declare personal bankruptcy to please your woman; you just have to be selective about what you get her. But remember that women have this strange ability to figure out how you feel about them by analyzing the meaning of gifts.

Find out what she wants

The trick here is to start your research before the day comes around. Do not wait until the last minute because you will only suffer for it.

Your girlfriend wants to be swept off her feet, not disappointed with a potpourri ensemble that you picked up at the corner store on your way home from work.

When you go out together, listen carefully to everything she says that could be of use. Put in the extra effort and pay attention because it will be useful in the long run. When she drags you shopping on the weekend, pay attention to what catches her eye. These window-shopping moments are the best for taking notes on upcoming gifts.

Another great way to find out crucial tidbits of info for the perfect gift is through family and friends. On top of the fact that you will be scoring extra points with her loved ones, you will also be getting insider information as to what she really wants.

Play detective

Remember that she won't spell it out for you, because that would simply defeat the purpose. She expects you to know her well enough to recognize what she would like.

The good thing here is that eventually your investigative efforts will get back to her. This means that you will be a two-time winner: Not only will you have found the perfect present, but she will also know how much you care because you went the extra mile to do the research, and this may lead to another winning situation . . .

In case you are lazy by nature, here are some surefire signs of love she will enjoy.

■ Photo album

Giving her a photo album shows that you see a future for both of you and that you want to build something with her. Putting in a few pictures of both of you is a great way to start the photo collection.

■ Compilation of her favorite songs

This simple gift signifies how much you value your time together, and the songs represent the different aspects of your life together.

■ Spa retreat for two

What your girlfriend enjoys most is spending time alone with you. Make her day with a getaway for two at an out-of-town health spa where you will both be able to get a complete body makeover.

■ Tickets for a show

Treat her to the theater or a concert of her choice. Show her that you know what she likes, even if it may not necessarily be what you like.

■ Bed and breakfast

Time well spent is quality time together. This simple time away from home allows her to observe a new environment and experience new things. Although it might only be spending it in a country house and going for a calm walk in the woods, these moments count for a lot.

The most important thing—and this can't be overstressed—is to get her something that either represents her uniqueness or that the two of you can enjoy together.

GUIDE TO ANNIVERSARIES

Not all anniversaries are created equal. Indeed, different anniversaries call for different types of celebrations. But you don't have to plan for weeks to have a great celebration; you just have to do two things: remember the date (yes, mark it in your calendar), and heed AskMen.com's advice as you plan that perfect night.

1. The three-month anniversary

What it means: For most couples, the three-month mark is the time to realize that they're headed for a committed relationship. So, you can approach this celebration as your opportunity to mutually acknowledge your commitment to each other.

What you should do: You can opt for the traditional meal out. Pick a snazzy place and get yourself looking sharp. Remember: Play this celebration as a toast to the future rather than one to the past. Or as an alternative to the regular dinner, consider planning a fun event. Take her to a comedy show or a concert that she'll like; this way, you can spend time together without too much seriousness. (Note: Three months is the earliest you should celebrate. Celebrate any earlier and you may come off as overeager.)

2. The one-year anniversary

What it means: The one-year mark signifies that you've overcome the beginning stages of a relationship and you still want to be together beyond that. From her perspective, she'll see the day as a time to remember all your "firsts" together (first date, first kiss).

What you should do: Pull out the cheesiness and get sappy for your lady. This celebration is a pure homage to your year spent together. One good way to mark it as such is to build it around mementos of your time together—drink the same wine you had on your first date or listen to the same CD you had playing the first time you kissed. Also, show her you remember all the fun times you've spent together during the past year by taking her to a great restaurant you've been to or on a picnic somewhere memorable (cheesy, yes, but it should have the desired effect). Or if you want to go big, consider planning a night or a weekend out of town.

3. The two-year anniversary

What it means: You're past the point of celebrating "firsts." At the two-year mark, you should show her how much you appreciate her.

What you should do: Think of the two-year mark as her very own Valentine's Day, because this anniversary is more about her. This is a time to demonstrate your gratitude for all the great things she's done for you. Package it in the form of an experience you can share together; ideally, it will be something she's been talking about for the past two years (skydiving, whitewater rafting, or a short road trip). This can even be the start of a ritual activity for you to do on future anniversaries. For the two-year mark and beyond, don't forget to buy her a gift. This could be anything from jewelry (usually the preferred choice) to gift certificates for massages and other pampering.

4. The five-year mark and beyond

What it means: You're in it for the long haul.

What you should do: By now, you're probably in the groove of anniversaries. You probably know what she expects and you may even have your own ritual. At this point, your families may even be involved in the celebration, planning, and gift buying (yes, you have to do that again). So what's the challenge after five years? Just remembering the date is the hard part.

And just because many anniversary celebrations have come and gone at this point, don't let them become a routine. Try to aim for something special every year (if you're running low on creative ideas, you're allowed to recycle celebration activities from past years—just add a different twist to them). The worst thing you can do is to ignore anniversaries as the years go on; they should always be acknowledged and celebrated. If you take this advice and put in just a little bit of effort, she'll be singing your praises to her friends and family until next year.

SPICING UP YOUR SEX LIFE

Now that we've addressed the necessary rituals to be respected in relationships, let's shift our focus to introducing new elements into your relationship to keep it interesting. The appropriate venue for many such introductions is the bedroom. The appropriate occasions for them, however, can vary, and this variance should be encouraged in the interest of spontaneity.

All too often, established couples don't even consider initiating a lovemaking session outside of the regular schedule that they have become accustomed to. However, there are a number of occasions in which you wouldn't expect your girl to be gazing longingly at you, but these are actually great opportunities to add some spontaneity to your sex life. Yes, unexpected sex can and does happen—especially if you take advantage of those brief moments to grab hold of her. You'll be surprised to find out when a woman feels desirable. Try your luck at some of the following situations and see what happens. You may just find yourself getting it on when you least expect it.

After exercise

Clearing the cobwebs out via a good workout makes a woman feel powerful and sexy. She may walk into the gym feeling like the world's biggest pig, but you can guarantee she will walk out tall as a sunflower and feeling like a million bucks. A workout has a number of mood-enhancing physiological effects, and a woman in a good mood is ready for it.

First, exercise releases endorphins that make girls feel happy. Second, a good workout helps detoxify the body from the inside out via the lymphatic system, making all body systems function more effectively—including the reproductive side of things. Third, your girl is doing something positive for her body; she doesn't have to feel guilty anymore for the cakes she ate or if she hasn't been to the gym for a month.

Everything is absolved when she walks out that door. So when she walks through your door in her sweatpants, take advantage of her high spirits and her endorphin-laden body. Any form of exercise has these effects to varying degrees, so even going for a brisk walk will help get her blood flowing to all those special places.

What not to do: She also may have been at work all day prior to her exercise, so she might not want you to go near her if she's not feeling fresh. Depending on your own preference and hers, it may be best to wait until she has had a shower before getting too close, but watch out: The moment might have passed by then!

When she's angry

Aggression is a strange but powerful aphrodisiac. Ever wonder why make-up sex is so good? Being fired up gets her aggressive side going, and aggressive women love sex. The trouble with angry sex is that if she's mad at you—which, let's face it, is highly likely—she isn't going to want to let you win by having sex with you. It is a juxtaposition that she will find highly confusing—her desire undermines her by making her want you even more than she normally does, but if she were to follow through on this desire, she would be voiding the argument.

What not to do: Don't ever assume that she is going to be angry and frisky at the same time. If she is, more often than not, she will never confess this to you—that would be an unnecessary liability!

Trying to get it on at this time will probably land you a big fat slap on the cheek, and that's only if you're lucky, because it could be worse—especially if she is bad-tempered. Always use your common sense when dealing with an angry woman.

When she's all dolled up

You wouldn't expect her to want to be ruffled at this time for fear of ruining all her hard work. Not always so: She will be feeling exceptionally foxy at this time, especially if she is looking forward to the day or night ahead, and this can make her feel daring and sexy.

Having enough time to relax with a glass of wine before going out is a useful approach—being late won't do, and neither will trying to get it on when she is half-ready. This one may take planning.

What not to do: Be careful not to mess her up too much, for the simple reason that she will make you late by having to fix herself up again. And we all know how tedious it is waiting for chicks to put their war paint on and get out the door. She will also think you are considerate and thoughtful for not being absentminded when it comes to her carefully applied decorations—this is always a benefit and works well for future favors.

The important thing is to keep your sex life exciting for both of you, so don't be afraid to get creative!

WOO HER ALL OVER AGAIN

Obviously, one of the biggest obstacles any long-term relationship faces is the disheartening possibility that the heat might suddenly disappear. One day, you're a hot couple that sneaks quickies on your lunch break; the next, you're the stereotypical "boring couple" that has a lovemaking schedule and eats at the same restaurant every Saturday night because "the food is always hot and it's not so expensive." The feeling is palpable when the attraction starts to fade, and it can seriously hinder a relationship, whether you've been together for two years or twenty.

Therefore, there will come a time when you need to step up and make your special lady feel special all over again. When you spotted that breathless beauty across the room, you were probably the first to wander over with your awkward opening line. Well, you should find new ways to make that courageous trek all over again. The trick is making her believe she's that same nervous yet excited girl who watched you approach with bated breath.

We've put together a list of ideas that can help you rekindle lost passion in your relationship; at the very least, it will prove that there are ways to postpone boredom and revive old feelings.

Re-create the first few days of your relationship

It's not about a simple anniversary. It's not about one day in the early phases of your dating. It's about reliving those wonderful sensations both of you experienced during the first few encounters. Granted, it won't be easy, but that doesn't mean the attempt won't have the desired effect. Once you embark on re-experiencing—not reenacting—those first feelings of interest and attraction, you will be surprised at how rejuvenating those emotions can be. It's those feelings that should be the focal point of the experiment; your goal is to refresh the current status of your relationship.

You can set up a faux blind date. Arrange to meet each other at a location neither of you have visited in the past, and seek to experience a second first date. You can even introduce yourselves all over again, attempt new topics of conversation, and generally proceed as if you're seeing each other for the very first time. Again, the attempt alone should provide the necessary spark.

Fight the aging process by staying active

Whether you are in your late twenties or late forties, when you're involved in a long-term relationship you might start to feel as if you're slowing down. But believe it or not, there really is something to the old saying, "You're only as young as you feel." You need to find a physical activity you can do together; not only will it keep you both moving, but it will also get the blood pumping a bit—and that's a good thing in more ways than one. Try going for a little hike every week, or taking tennis or racquetball. Whatever you choose, it will both maintain your health, and bring you closer together.

And let's say, for the sake of argument, that both of you want to lose a few pounds. Well, working out is tough, and misery loves company, so while she hits the treadmill, you can hit the rowing machine. The couple that sweats together bonds together, even outside the bedroom.

Be the exact opposite

It's just for a little while, and it doesn't mean that you should transform into a jerk just because you've always been a decent guy. It simply means that you should show her a side of you she's not familiar with. For example, you could reveal a previously hidden talent, tell her a story she's never heard, or become a hopeless romantic when you're usually the guy who forgets birthdays. One of the biggest passion killers is the onset of tedious predictability, so give her something she couldn't possibly predict. When working to infuse new passion into a relationship, rediscovering your partner is crucial.

It doesn't matter if your "unpredictable" side is the ability to juggle. It doesn't matter if you can tie eighteen different kinds of knots. Whatever you reveal to her, what ultimately matters is that she's never seen or heard it before.

Talk and listen

It may sound generic and even arbitrary, but it truly isn't. You may have noticed that you don't talk to each other as much as you used to; when you first began dating, you'd chat into the wee hours of the morning. Now, not so much. You could be immensely surprised at just how responsive she will be—in more than one way—if you simply ask her about her day and touch her gently on the shoulder. The little things tend to be forgotten as a relationship wears on, and the dinner discussion might eventually become borderline obligatory. This is exactly the kind of thing you're countering with this tip; make yourself available when she really needs to be heard. It's not arbitrary, it's essential, and it really is this simple.

Show her you appreciate her

She does a lot of things for you, and if there's one burden women often shoulder, it's that of being taken for granted. When she does even the smallest thing to help—something as simple as doing the laundry—make a point of giving her a meaningful "thank you." You can even try a dozen roses with a card that doesn't say, "I love you," but, "I appreciate you." She might need a day entirely to herself during which she isn't burdened by anything on the home front; you could spring for a day at the spa or a package deal at the salon. The point is that she's been doing so much for you, and now it's time for you to do something specifically for her.

Be playful and let her know she's irresistible

One of the most entertaining and revealing things a couple can do is play games, and we don't mean Monopoly. Leave sexy notes around the house, act playful and coy, and watch her react with giggles and warmth. You have to keep her on her toes, regardless of how long you have been together, and doing things like this will keep you in her mind. She'll also feel wanted, which isn't just a bonus, it's an absolute necessity.

In addition to feeling she's being taken for granted, she may also feel like she's not as attractive as she once was. You know she's still that breathtaking, gorgeous seductress who rocked the bed; the important thing is for her to know this. If you think that she's starting to feel a bit insecure, it's time to make her feel like a sexy woman all over again.

Wow your woman

You can easily utilize some of the tips here to really "wow" your woman if you sense that things are getting a little stale. It's simply a matter of observation; after you've recognized that things might be cooling off, it's up to you to take the initiative. One of the worst things you can do is to ignore the "cooling off" and attribute it to the typical occurrences of a long-term relationship; if you wait too long, even these helpful hints may not be enough. Don't let it get that far. You're capable, charming, virile, and above all, you still love her to death. It's time for her to know it.

8 WAYS TO REKINDLE ROMANCE

It happens in the best of relationships: What began with an endless parade of roses, chocolate, and five-hour lovemaking sessions has somehow turned into dried flowers, a thick waist, and robotic sex. The flames of passion seem to be slowly dying out.

True, it does become increasingly difficult to keep the momentum going after several years together, as bills, stress, and so forth can put your love life on the back burner. But the sizzle doesn't have to fizzle once you've settled down together.

Re-igniting that old spark is crucial to keep the relationship fresh and healthy (that is, it makes her feel the way she did when you first met), so here are eight great ways to do just that.

Number 8: Plan a surprise date

Throw her off-guard and sweep her off her feet with an unexpected rendezvous. This includes transforming the house into a lovers' paradise (rose petals and all), or slipping a blindfold on her and taking her to a secret location (a night at the opera, or a small intimate restaurant on the other side of town). Show her that you're still an unpredictable romantic.

Number 7: Get nostalgic

Look at old photos, read old letters, and relive special dates to stir up those feelings and emotions—including those initial "highs"—you felt when you first met, which may have simmered down as of late.

Number 6: Redecorate

Give your relationship a fresh start with a fresh coat of paint. That's right; try giving your bedroom a whole new look (out with the old, in with the new) and buy new bed sheets (no Spider-Man) and, if you can afford it, new furniture. Making the room more inviting (i.e., romantic) will not only impress her, it'll also give you an incentive to spend more time in your love nest.

Number 5: Get away

While you're at it, pack your bags, leave your worries at home, and take that long overdue trip to some romantic destination (a tropical haven like Hawaii or Fiji will not disappoint). Whether you're revisiting an old destination or heading toward a new romantic getaway, a little R&R might be just what the doctor ordered.

Even if you just don't have the time, you should at least allow yourselves one weekend of uninterrupted bliss.

Number 4: Get fresh

Re-energize your lovemaking sessions by getting a little more risqué in the bedroom. Whether it involves sexy board games, costumes, or some titillating manuals, becoming more provocative will put a fresh spin on a partner you've come to know well.

Number 3: Try something new

Find yourselves a new hobby, a chance for the two of you to spend time together in a new environment. You can try a painting, dancing, or even a cooking class, just as long as there is interaction, contact, and the opportunity to teach each other.

Number 2: Leave her alone

Strange but true: One of the best ways to nurture a relationship is by giving each other some alone time. After several years, your personal lives often become one, and so doing things on your own will not only make you appreciate seeing each other, but it will also give you new material to talk about as you tell each other what you've been up to. Remember that absence does make the heart grow fonder.

Number 1: Look ahead

Start mapping out how you plan to spend the rest of your lives together, whether it involves getting married, having children, or seeing the world. She may be impressed by the fact that you are taking initiative and are fully dedicated to the relationship, which will surely translate into an increase in romantic vibes.

Keep the passion alive

Don't let time put out the fire that burned when you first met. Reach back into the old days and pick out all the things that made the romance quirky and fun, from being more unpredictable and keeping her on her toes to becoming more active in each other's lives.

Going back to the old days will not only teach the two of you to love all over again, it will also remind you why you got together in the first place.

RULE 11
PLAN AHEAD

The deeper you progress into a relationship, the more serious the questions facing you and your woman will become. But you'll also find that you'll come to a consensus on many of them more easily—after all, you're much more familiar with each other's goals and values by now, and many of the bigger issues will have been addressed already.

One point of debate that is likely to persist, however, concerns marriage. To most women, a long-term relationship isn't perfect until the acquisition of one thing: a ring. And if you're not ready for the big walk down the aisle, you're going to have to do some pretty fast talking to avoid it.

POSTPONE YOUR PROPOSAL

For many, there are only two ways a relationship can ultimately turn out: marriage or breakup. If you're in a successful long-term relationship, the next step is usually seen to be a wedding.

However, not all couples come to this point at the same time. Often one craves and pressures for marriage before the other. To be put in this position is a true dilemma. Refusal to marry can cause problems in an otherwise sound relationship: She could think you're commitment-phobic, on the lookout for someone else, or just not all that serious about her.

But (hopefully) she's wrong. You're with her, happy with her, but just not ready to walk down the aisle . . . yet. We won't tell you how to dupe a girl into staying in a dead-end relationship, but here are a few strategies to help you postpone the proposal.

Enjoy the relationship first

Once you're married, you can expect big changes. You aren't a couple of adolescents fooling around—now you're man and wife. Along with this comes responsibility, starting a family, and settling down. Not that these are bad things, but they are big things. Big, scary, serious things.

Buy yourself more time by suggesting that the two of you really enjoy the relationship you have before moving on to more. Before you marry, take time to travel, go out on the town, and spend all your spare money and time having fun. A few more years of fun can help build a good solid foundation for a marriage.

Of course, once you are married, you'll have to accept all the changes you've delayed. But these should be part of the reason you decide to get married. This way, your girl will know that once you take the plunge, you will be ready for the realities of grown-up, family life.

Waiting for better circumstances

Given that marriage is the start of a new life with the woman you love, it should be the best possible one you can give her. Many couples jump into marriage without a penny to their name and find that love isn't really enough when they're in a real relationship in the real world. Working constantly to afford a tiny apartment and a couple of kids—is that really what your wife deserves?

Suggest that you hold back from marriage until your circumstances are more favorable. If you're in college, wait until you've graduated. If either of you have a promotion in sight, work towards that, because it will make married life easier in the long run. You can wait to get married until after you have a better apartment or house.

Explain to her that you don't want to get married if nothing is really going to change. By suggesting these material improvements to her, you are promising that marriage will lead to a better life, not just the same old relationship except for the one day of partying and the new ring.

Waiting for a better wedding

There are times the above strategy won't work. Your career, house, and circumstances could be pretty much established. Or she may insist that none of that is important to her and really wants to marry now. To postpone this, dangle a bigger and better wedding in front to her.

Your wedding day is supposed to be the happiest day of your life. It needs enough time, money, and organization to be perfect for the two of you. Tell her there's no point rushing to the wedding if you spend all day wishing you'd done it some other way. The perfect location, the dress that makes her look amazing, and a fantastic reception that all your friends and family can attend—surely that's better than a quick and cheap ceremony?

With the spiraling cost of weddings, this could buy you quite a lot of time . . . but at a price.

Wait for an important date

Holding the wedding on a meaningful date is a romantic and sentimental gesture. It can also push the ceremony well into the future. Claiming you want to get married on a birthday—hers or yours—or on the anniversary of your parents' wedding, or on a significant date for your relationship will get you an extra few months.

If you need more time, make the time of the anniversary important as well. Instead of marrying on the next Valentine's Day, ask to wait until it's the fifth or tenth one you've celebrated together. To make this idea more palatable, choose a date that is important to her—you have more chance with her parents' wedding anniversary than one commemorating your high school sporting victory.

Moral objection

To some people, marriage is the ultimate goal of a relationship; to others, it's completely pointless. Telling your girl that you don't want to get married can feel like a rejection to her. The blow can be softened by explaining that you reject the whole idea of marriage and that if you did believe in it, of course you'd do it with her.

"I don't need a piece of paper to show I love you" may be a cliché, but it's a view that many people share. However, just as many believe that marriage is essential. If you use this approach, and then discover that to her, marriage is a deal-breaker, you could find the relationship is in trouble.

Honesty

If she is particularly determined to marry, the above approaches may not work. In this case, straight talking is in order. Explain to her that marriage is a huge step and you want to wait until you are 100% ready for it.

Stress that when you do get married, it's going to be forever—you don't want something that you'll back out of after a couple of years. It's important to take things at their own pace and not rush into a commitment one of you isn't ready for.

Throughout this, let her know that you aren't on the lookout for something or someone better. You aren't ruling out marriage forever, just for the moment. You will have to make the extra effort in the relationship to make her feel better about this and to "apologize" for not being ready.

Marriage is a big deal, for men and for women. If you spend all your time trying to dodge the bullet, think carefully. Take all the time you need, but avoid stringing her along. By postponing for the right reasons, you make sure that when you do eventually marry, it's the happiest day for both of you.

TOP 10 SIGNS YOU'RE READY TO POP THE QUESTION

Contrary to popular belief, most guys want to get married . . . eventually. It may take us longer to recognize the symptoms of marriage-itis, but it's there, nonetheless. Sharing our lives with one woman, having steady sex for life, and the possibility of kids does cross our minds.

Have a look at the top ten things that should alert you to the fact that you might want to "make an honest woman" out of your current belle.

Number 10: You want to settle down

Feeling like the pace of single life is too hectic? Do you look at your single friends as if they're all just running around pointlessly from party to party with no greater ambition than to find their next "lay"? More important, have you caught yourself contemplating whether there's something more? There is, and your gut tells you the answer lies with your girlfriend. This is a telltale indicator that you're well on your way to accepting the inevitable . . . marriage. What once was a taboo subject has become a most reasonable idea. The only real dilemma now is how you break this revelation to your friends. Yeah, you'll take some good-natured ribbing from your buds, but in the end, you'd trade in that pool cue for your honey any day of the week.

Number 9: You want to experience life with her

Now that you've been together for a while, you begin to realize that she's someone very special. Whenever you go out of town on business, you frequently wish she could be there with you. Conversely, when she's away, it hits you that you can't wait for her to get back. You want to vacation with her and visit new places together. In other words, you've reached a point where you can't picture her ever leaving your life and you see yourself growing old with her. Face the facts, pal, you're headed toward marriage alley and you actually like the idea.

Number 8: You love her quirks

In past relationships, you've always ended up being annoyed by your girlfriends' little habits. Whether it was a constant need for shopping sprees or leaving her hair all over your bathroom, there was always something you could not get over—but not with this one. The way she teases you playfully or makes fun of your complete collection of Pittsburgh Steeler bobble heads, in your eyes, is all good. In fact, you find yourself laughing along with her more often than not. This is a clear indication of how much you've come to appreciate her character.

Number 7: You consider her family your own

You've met her parents and she's met yours. You've weathered holidays, birthdays, barbecues, and perhaps even the occasional tragedy together with her family. As they have embraced you as someone important in your girlfriend's life, so too have you come to care for them more than any other group of people (with the exception of your own kin, of course). When you get this intertwined with her, there's only one place left to go.

Number 6: You already know what ring to buy her

So you've started looking at diamonds and rings? Surely this must mean that you've been paying some attention to your lady's hints. Even more amazing to you, this is a process that feels less like a "chore" and more like a labor of love. You want the ring to really reflect your taste and your commitment to her. If this doesn't tell you you're ready to propose, then . . . what exactly are you doing it for?

Number 5: You imagine all the good times surrounding the wedding

It's all becoming an exciting prospect to you, this idea of marriage. The fact that it doesn't scare you is remarkable. But more amazingly, you realize that you can spin a ton of positives out of it.

The wedding party will be a blast. Friends you haven't seen in a while will all be celebrating, drinking, and dancing with you again at your reception. Plus, this time you get to be the recipient of a stag party and not merely a participant.

Number 4: You start sacrificing financially

Another clue that you're really ready to pop the question is when you've begun calculating the fees necessary to take a wife. You realize that you'll need to give up some luxuries in order to finance this event. A true man steps up and shows his woman that he's ready and able to field the cost.

If, for example, you sell the aforementioned bobble head collection to a dealer to get some cash or trade in your Audi for a fuel-efficient Toyota to save for the wedding (and you can smile while doing so), then you're ready. If you've recognized this need and, more important, are eager to make it happen, then you're in line to get hitched.

Number 3: You want her to be the mother of your children

This one's big. It may not have been that long ago when the mere thought of being a "daddy" sent you running for the nearest bottle of tequila. However, if being with your latest lady has you actually thinking of children's names and even grinning at the thought that she might be the mother to your brood, you've certainly got nuptials on the brain.

Number 2: You make long-term plans together

The realization that you're ready for marriage may actually be obvious. If you've initiated or willingly participated in discussions with your girl-friend about eventually buying a house, having children, saving for re-tirement, or any such future plans, then it's a logical assumption for you (and a fait accompli for her) that you should propose.

Similarly, if you've found yourself paying special attention to reports about the suburbs (hikes in taxes, school zones, housing markets, etc.), then don't fight it any longer, you're ready.

Number 1: You know she's the one

While all the prior examples are good indicators of readiness for mar-riage, nothing is as important as this one. In essence, this reason is really the sum of all prior indicators; it's the reason why all signs point to her. After all, you're with her now for a reason. She is the culmination of all the dating experiences that came before.

You've learned who you are, you remember the girls you've thrown back while waiting for that special catch. And now you know that the "one" is in your life. All her good traits and the way she makes you feel about yourself impress upon you the absolute need to keep this one. There was never anyone like her in your life before and you know there won't be again. So stop dilly-dallying and get to it, man.

Go make her yours

If your head and your heart have been giving off any or all of the above signals, you're probably ready to ask your lady to marry you. And don't think she hasn't noticed your change in demeanor, either. Women are intuitive—any "out of the ordinary" behavior would have been duly noted on her boyfriend radar. But rest assured, she's probably happily awaiting your "surprise."

Your journey down life's shared road is only four words away. Now be a man and go make the love of your life the happiest woman in the world.

PROPOSAL PROTOCOL

A handful of rituals, repeated time and again, help to define the marriage proposal, but they amount to neither sacrament nor formula; at best, they present a framework. The details are up to you, and once you've decided to pop the question, you'll learn that posterity is peeking down on you, curious to see what makes your proposal, if not timeless, at least memorable.

To that end, there are lots of ways to do this right and have it remembered fondly, but many more to do it wrong—so wrong it either becomes an extended family joke you can never escape from if she says "yes," or it serves as a sad, cautionary tale to others if she says "no." In between right and wrong is a big gray area, the boneyard of forgettable proposals, where the bland and uninspired methods go to die.

A marriage proposal is one of those requisite stories she'll be telling her friends and family about when asked how you proposed. If you infuse the following protocol with your own imaginative details, you can give her a story she can be proud of, one she'll enjoy retelling for years afterwards—a dynamite proposal story to make her friends jealous and her enemies disgusted.

Proposal rules and etiquette

Inform her parents beforehand

The key word here is *inform*, not ask, and you should be cautious that your language reflects as much. You can ask for their permission, but you're not beholden to it if they don't approve; after all, by allowing her father to say "no," you deny her the basic ability to make her own choices.

On the other hand, it's good manners to involve them in the process, since for them it may suggest at least token involvement in their daughter's life. While this may seem old-fashioned, in this case and elsewhere, give tradition the benefit of the doubt.

Naturally, there are some exceptional circumstances that would dictate a different course. If she's estranged from her parents, she hasn't spoken to them in a number of years, or they are not a part of her life, informing them is not necessary.

On that note, any plans or schemes you might be harboring of using the proposal to bring them all together are ill-advised and should be abandoned.

Do not involve her in the choice of the ring

Doing so would be catastrophic to at least two key elements of a great proposal: surprise and romance.

If you have discussed marriage at some point prior to your proposal, then you should have ascertained what she wants in an engagement ring. If you haven't, you're left to your memory and your wits—not the most reliable things in the world. Whether it's been discussed or not, you should consider enlisting a sibling, relative, or close friend of hers to help you out, one whom you trust.

Give careful consideration to your stage

This is basic: Gear the venue around her tastes and her personality. If you know she would savor an audience, the bigger the better, make sure there is one. If not, practice some discretion: The bigger the stage, the bigger the stakes. While uncertainty on your part shouldn't overly influence your choice of venue, you're more likely to get a pressured and later retracted "yes" at a crowded stadium on the Jumbo-tron.

Additionally, you want a venue conducive to the moment after. You don't want to catch her at a stressful time of the day, or at a time when she can't enjoy it.

Give it a formal tone

In other words, don't be casual; this is a formal marriage proposal and it requires a degree of formality on your part, beginning with how you ask. You'll be nervous, but that won't excuse throw-offs like "wanna get married?" or "I ain't getting on one knee." Stick to "Will you marry me?"

Formality applies to the traditional gesture of the bended knee as well, although there's a bit of flexibility here. If the occasion suits it—meaning you're in a place that physically allows for it, you know she'll appreciate it and might even be expecting it—bend down onto your left knee and say your piece. The gesture is old-fashioned—some might even call it cheesy—but it has a romantic flair, and at the very least you should give it proper consideration.

Be prepared for any answer

Meaning both "yes," "no," *and* "I need to think about it."

This may not seem fair, but this process has afforded you plenty of time to make the decision to propose; consequently, she deserves equal time if she needs it. Every man wants a resounding "yes," but not every man will get it, no matter how the proposal is done.

Be present for her reaction

Some of the more extreme or elaborate proposal ideas floating around the Internet ultimately result in your lady being asked by billboards, computers, and blimps. While there's nothing automatically wrong with this, no matter what the plan, when the question is popped you need to be with her, period.

Take a unique approach

Finally, tailor your approach to her, and to your relationship. Give it a context. In other words, riding in on a white horse under 100 pounds of chain mail is only romantic if there's some greater relevance to it; otherwise, it's unimaginative and stereotypical. Spending hundreds of dollars on an elaborate proposal with "the works" makes little sense if a well-written poem would better contextualize your relationship.

A proposal of marriage is a serious matter, but the proposal itself doesn't need to be so serious; it can be fun, romantic, wild, or all three. In the final analysis, if your proposal features little beyond a ring and a question, you can still do it right—you can still give her a story to tell—you can still earn a "yes"—if you infuse it with meaning. With your heart. The more elaborate the proposal, the more things that can go wrong, and the greater the chance you stray from the fundamental goal: asking the woman you love to marry you and to spend the rest of her life with you.